Intro

Hello, and welcome to <u>Dark Beer and Taco Tuesdays</u>! A collection of stories that I find summarizes my mind quite well. This project perhaps above all others in the past, was a true labour of love. Every single story in this collection was written with someone or multiple someones in mind. Whether it's a close friend, family member, mentor or just grand influence on my style, each of these tales has a certain importance to me. In truth quite a few of these were difficult to write. By nature I'm not the most outwardly emotional of men, with the emotional side of myself being something that only people that I consider the best of companions see. For these stories however, I had to do away with that notion and bring up certain things that I had avoided thinking about for quite some time, whether it's a lost friendship or a lost life.

Enough with the dramatism though, and let me give you a little background on the stories that you're about to read, or you're at least thinking about reading if you've gotten this far. The title of the collection is blunt, in fact it's not artistic in the slightest, but is perhaps the most important influence on anything I write. Dark beer and Tex-Mex cuisine for cheap prices, I love both like they were my own edible family. Those two things, often found in combination with one another are where the vast majority of my ideas flourished from. I couldn't even attempt to count how much nonsense came into my head

Dark Beer & Taco Tuesdays

while eating some delicious $4 giant tacos, or downing a delicious brew as dark as the midnight sky on Queen Street, Niagara Falls, which in its most distilled form is what this collection is a tribute to.

There was a point in time where I would consider myself my most prolific that you could find me nearly every day of the week wandering the streets of downtown Niagara Falls, taking in the cold, or heat, or whatever nonsensical weather that seemed to change on a daily basis. Bars became my second home, and the only reason you don't still find me down there so often is because I ran out of the funds to do so.

There's a lot more than just alcoholism that fueled this collection though, for the best part of downtown isn't the beer, or even the immaculate bar food, but the people, the majestic pedestrians that fill my life with a joy that I had never really known before. Downtown is the first time that I felt like a true part of a community since high school concert band, which I'm sure will have its own collection in due time. As a man that at one point in his life couldn't leave his own home due to fear of persecution, the people of downtown Niagara Falls opened their arms to me and immediately came to see me as another fixture in the community. It was through observing and receiving their jovial attitudes and occasionally grumpy demeanours that I came into my own, and I learned for the first time that I was a pretty big fan of myself, something that I once thought would never come into my mind.

Anyhow, that'll about do it for the mushy stuff. Let's get weird, shall we?

Dark Beer & Taco

Tuesdays: Volume 1

By Erik Upper

ISBN: 978-0-9947380-2-8
Cover made in part by Thomas O'Neil
Copyright Frozen Harbour Press
Originally Printed: June 2, 2016

Editing assistance provided by –
Ryan McGratten - "Steve"
Julian Yager – "Lion in the Lurch"
Robert Cole – "Matthias Gulgod and the Cult of the Grave Wizard"
Josh Johnson – "Saltman"
Katherine Upper – "Guided"
Ashleigh Kandas – "Orthopraxy: In the Beginning"

The author would like to give his outmost thanks to all those that provided assistance on this collection.

Dark Beer & Taco Tuesdays

This volume is dedicated to Sarah, the greatest sister a fellow could ask for. Thanks for first inspiring me to start writing, and teaching me how to drink, haha! Love ya!

Table of Contents

Steve – An Attempt to Write Something for Children

Something that very few people know about me is that I'm a fan of children, from baby to teenager, there's something to marvel about when it comes to the fact that these are smaller human beings whose minds and bodies are literally forming into a person right in front of me. At this point in my life is seems a bit doubtful that I'll be having children any time in the near future, despite fatherhood being one of the major goals in my life.

The story that you're about to read is almost an ode to my future child, based around the absurdity and surrealism that I myself like to perpetrate in everyday life. It's a rather short story, but it took a surprising amount of effort to put together. The first draft actually included a decapitation, but I figured that might not be the best choice for the audience it's directed to.

I'm pretty happy with this first attempt to write something for kids, though I might come back to it another day and build on it a bit more. Who knows, by the end of this grand adventure I could be a young adult author (let's hope not, for the sake of the children.)

Children's Story – Steve

This story was inspired by Roddy, Cowan, Tristan, and all the other fantastic children of my friends that I can't wait to see develop into super beings.

Children's Story – Steve

The ogre looked down at Steve, "A bit small aren't you? Sure you don't want to run back home before you find yourself lost?"

"Watch your tongue, foul green giant! I am Steve, the bravest, strongest and wisest man from my village!" Steve tapped the ogre's leg with his walking stick. "Now be on your way creature, unless you want to taste my revenge!"

The ogre's belly shook as he laughed, "You've got a lot of spirit in you, boy. I'll give you that!" With a mighty burp the ogre stood aside, letting Steve pass. As he watched Steve cross his path the ogre gave Steve a pat on the back. What the ogre thought was a friendly tap on the shoulder managed to knock Steve to the ground, resulting in another belly shaking laugh. "My goodness, young man, if you can't handle a pat on the back from a friendly ogre then what hope do you have?!"

"Bah!" said Steve. "I can handle anything... You simply caught me unprepared." With that Steve gathered his belongings, which were now spread across the ground, and hurried onwards while the ogre laughed hard and heavy behind him.

It would be a few more minutes of walking until Steve came to the first house along the roadside. Looking for a place to sleep for the night Steve knocked on the door, he was too foolhardy to worry about the danger of strange people in a strange land. To his surprise a giraffe's head popped out of the cabin's chimney wearing giraffe sized sunglasses and a mouthful of leaves.

The giraffe mumbled a response through his mouth full of food, "Hirrol, uw an I halp you?"

"I'm sorry?" replied Steve.

The sunglasses wearing giraffe gave a few quick chews and swallowed his food. "My apologies, my dear fellow, allow me to introduce myself. My name is Spotsworth the Bespectacled, a giraffe of fine repute in these parts. Now, if you would be so kind to supply me with your name, good sir."

"Ah, I am pleased to meet a creature of such good manners in this part of the world! My name is Steve, a great adventurer. I was looking for a place to stay for the night and wondered if you would have any space available for a tired sort of fellow like me."

"By the good grace's feeble moustache, has no one told you to beware of strangers? This is an odd place, with poor standing in the world! I could have let you in and devoured you whole if I had felt the want to do so! Though in truth I am a giraffe of peace, I know little and less about you, good lad, so to your request I say, of course not! However, I will lend you my giraffe tent and neck cozy, which should fit you well." Spotsworth the Bespectacled popped his head back into his cabin, and after a few minutes of loud rumblings and tumblings popped back out with a number of devices on his head. "Here you are, sir." Spotsworth tossed the tent and neck cozy to Steve. "I shall be expecting those back sometime soon. Goodbye, adventurer," with that Spotsworth returned to his cabin.

"Bah!" said Steve. "What a strange giraffe, though I suppose the tent will do well enough for now."

As Steve slept he dreamed of stinky werebears, bumpy roads and being tied to a big stick. Unfortunately for Steve, those weren't dreams at all, and upon awakening in a smelly werebear cave at the side of a bumpy road and tied to a giant stick, this became obvious. Steve had had quite a few encounters with werebears in the past however, so he was far from afraid.

A voice came from behind him, "Hello, wereman, how are you feeling?"

"I am just dandy, beast. Now untie me and let me on my way. I have no time for your kind's foolishness today." The creature made his way into Steve's view. The beast was dressed in pajamas, a bath robe and slippers, though the slipper's toes had been torn through by his giant toenails. He was the hairiest werebear Steve had ever seen, near the entirety of the creature's skin was covered in long hair, but in all honesty though, he was very well groomed.

5

Children's Story – Steve

"You are making quite a bit of noise in this part of the world, human boy. Near every troll, ogre, owl-bear, snake-bear, monkey-bear and even goblin has heard of your appearance. As the wisest, smelliest and clearly best groomed creature in all these lands, you must tell me what it is you're here for."

It was of no use to fight the demands of a werebear, especially if everyone knew Steve was here already. "Fine, beast, I will tell you why I'm here. My great aunt Sylvia Longpants Firebeard Witchbottom recently bought some land out here, and I have been given the task of delivering her this jar of honey on behalf of my father."

"Ah, of course, I knew you reminded me of someone! Lucky for you your great aunt has become quite a good friend of my people over these past couple of weeks, for a free jar of honey sounds like a great proposition. In fact, out of the kindness of my well-groomed heart I will lead you to her cottage."

It would be another three days before Steve reached his great aunt's home. In this time Steve was forced to attend two werebear council meetings, which were composed primarily of grunts and scratching butts on trees. As they walked, more werebears joined up with them due to his guide's popularity, which led to Steve having to concentrate harder and harder to keep their beastly mitts off of his honey jar. In fact by the time they had reached Sylvia Longpants Firebeard Witchbottom's cabin, there were nearly 200 werebears with him.

To his surprise he found his great aunt sitting on the porch outside her cabin, sharing a pot of tea with none other than Spotsworth the Bespectacled, the giraffe he had met earlier in the journey.

"Ah, my good nephew Steve, I see you've made a few friends on your travels!"

"Yes, well great aunt, here is your honey as ordered. Now I will be taking my leave." With that Steve turned around and started to head back home as his great aunt, Spotsworth and the nearly 200 werebears stared at him in disbelief.

"I suppose you don't have my tent do you?" asked Spotsworth. Without turning around or even stopping Steve simply pointed to the lead werebear, who was still dressed in his pajamas. "Ah, see Sylvia, this is why I just can't trust strangers."

"Well, he always was a strange lad." Steve's great aunt motioned for the werebears to come inside. "Let's break open the honey, shall we?" the huge collection of werebears cheered in delight.

Though the journey to his aunt's house had lasted four days, the journey back to his starting path took less than two by just following the main road. Steve grumbled at the idea of all the time he had wasted, and vowed to never return to this place again.

Lion in the Lurch – An Ode to the Fellow that I'm Blessed to call my Best Friendo

Out of perhaps all my friendships, it is my one with Mr. McGratten that I've found to be the most captivating and simultaneously the most perplexing. For a long time I spent my life with the mindset that the importance of one's friends is based around how long you've been close companions. Though I never used this as a rule of who to give trust to, or who to spend most of my time with, I couldn't help but believe there was some truth in it. I mean, it's only logical that friendships are based around the idea of becoming used to another's presence.

While there have been a number of moments in my life that this idea was put to the test, the idea became truly dissolved when the magnificent presence of the Ryman himself entered my life with the force of a thousand suns. The two of us had actually known of each other's presence for quite a while, near a decade, and while we always respected each other and enjoyed the rare occasion that our paths would cross, it was not until little over a year ago at the time of this writing that our friendship grew, when we were brought together over a St. Patrick's Day gig in London concocted by a mutual friend.

Over that short course of a little over half a week I learned of something magical, that this man, despite always being in contact with him, was, to sum it up in an underrated fashion, my hero. He proved to be both everything I adored in myself, and much more. It would only be a matter of weeks until the two of us began hanging out nearly twice a week, and in the year that we've been compadres I can honestly say that I have developed more as a human being than I could've possibly imagined.

Here's to you, you gentlest of gents, you saltiest of salt cods and you sauciest of sauce pans.

Out of all the stories I've ever written this was perhaps the easiest to compose, pumping out the finished, edited copy in less than a week. It concerns a British admiral during the Napoleonic wars, and is written in a rather droll style, emulating the folk writing of the early Victorian, or perhaps more accurately late Pyrate Age. As much as I enjoy the final version, which I do, I can't help but feel that its tributary nature of both the man that inspired it and the era that the writing style derives from just isn't up to proverbial snuff.

From as early as I can remember one of my favourite time periods has been the 18th century. Whether it's the philosophers, the scientists or the mariners, the 1700's was a time in history that anyone with an interest in the nature of the human condition can enjoy reading about. While this story itself takes place in a fictional representation of the early half of the century that followed, in all honesty it was just an excuse to use the Napoleonic Wars as a setting. The writing style and characters are far more representative of the early half of that beloved "Enlightenment".

Lion in the Lurch

Maritime business was tough in the 19th century; the ban on pirating had been enacted and brutally enforced. Those with salt in their blood were forced to take up on commercial vessels where the pay was about enough to cover a week's worth of living for a month's worth of work. This was better than the navy where the pay was even less and the danger twice as palpable. For most of the men though, the job wasn't about getting paid, but taking to the seas, their true homes, a place where the grimiest of characters could hide from the harsh realities of 1800's Britain into an even harsher alternative.

In 1848 a British whaling ship off the coast of Greenland is desperate for entertainment. The ports in Greenland offer little more than a bite to eat and a bit of rancid drink for the lads. It's been months since the boys had been home. Fearing a mutiny on his hands, the captain took it onto himself to try and remedy the situation by telling a story from his years in the navy. The story of one of the bravest men he'd ever seen.

"Ay, lads, let's calm ourselves, shall we? Look at the shape of you mangy dogs, you deserve better and more for the work you've put in to this vessel. Hell, look at the catches we made, you'd think the queen herself would be looking to dine on orca based on the demand."

An outburst of rage broke out amongst a few of the crew and a small fight ensued as a result. As they all sat in the crew quarters awaiting the end of the captain's daily address, they couldn't help but feel similar to used dish rags. Something that would be used and abused its whole life until it was merely tossed away and forgotten about as a relic of the past. Fights were happening on a daily basis because tensions were so damn high. Rage and sorrow, the only emotions that any of them felt anymore were holding hard on their souls, slowly crushing them from the inside out. Even the first mate, a man of irreparable devotion to his captain was starting to feel the tinge of mutiny flow through his bones.

"I'll tell you what, it ain't much, but let me tell you a story. I can guarantee you ain't heard this one before, and she'll tickle even the hardest man's fancy. She's a story of adventure, brutality, and hell, even a bit of the old romance. It's about a man from my navy days, when I was off in the seas as a lowly private under the command of the great Ryan Elmwood, or as you might know him, Ryan the Lion. We were fighting the forces of the whore of Europe himself, the dreaded Napoleon, when all this happened."

The men quieted down. They knew that the captain was once considered a great storyteller back in Wales where he came from, but he had given up that life, some say he ran away from it to the seas. Rumours had circulated amongst the crew, and even a few in the docks that the captain had told a tale to the queen herself once upon a time, but was unsatisfied with the work that he provided her and gave up stories ever since.

Through all their hardships they never truly blamed the captain for what had been occurring on the ship, even if he was a little lily livered for his own good. To many of the men he was the best captain they had ever come across, but still their difficulties in this voyage couldn't be ignored even if it was mostly due to bad luck.

The captain noticed the decorum and patience that the men were giving him and thanked them before he began.

It was 1812, the British naval forces were separated, for while the raging storm of the French seamen bombarded all of Europe that it could get its hands on, tensions in the colony of Canada had finally burst their bubble and the American filth had begun their assaults both by sea and land. Most of us sailors had dreamt that the war against the French would have ended years earlier, but as we all well know, it hadn't. The war in Canada was simply an eventuality, what with the aggression of American expansion that had been occurring since their revolution, and the fact that their allies the French had left their settlers in the colony out to dry. Seeing as offending the French was the only thing keeping them back, I suppose they figured that they might as well attack.

Most of us desired to stay in Europe, but there were some volunteers that took to Canada, those that preferred the wilderness and staking new land claims I suppose. Anyhow, I was one of the lucky ones and got to stay amongst the seas that I knew best. What I didn't get to stay amongst though, was the crew that I had grown to love being a part of, instead the higher ups told me that I was to be reassigned to a new ship. At the time I had no idea which ship it was going to be, and while reassignments certainly weren't uncommon, it had been a number of years since I was last given one, so I was a bit surprised. That surprise grew tenfold when I realized the ship that I was to be sent to was the HMS Plutarch, captained by none other than admiral Elmwood, the Lion of the British seas.

Admiral Ryan Elmwood was famous for a few things, one of the most notable being that he was the only admiral in her majesty's service that held no fleet. He preferred to travel with a lone vessel that just so happened to be the size of a cargo train and a blue whale mashed together, if you'll let me engage in a bit of hyperbole. Instead he commanded through the use of carrier pigeons, aside from when he was needed most for crucial battles, where you could always be expecting his Union Jack flying high on the sea, and his forty-eight cannons aimed to perfection on the very eyeball of his rival captains.

The Lion's crew was often hand-picked by the man himself, though on occasion an officer of high rank would choose amongst the best in the navy to join him, so how I got there I'll never know. Ah, ya find that funny, eh? Ya bunch of jammy buggers. Nah, I'm a bit hard on meself, I was a hell of a crewman back in the day, but compared to the men that I'd be sharing that ship with I was little more than a fly in the ointment. They included such great lads as; Brandonio the Bold, an Italian-Native American known for his great skills with a pistol, of which he always carried eight at a time; Thommy "Big Irish" Ua Neill, a handyman, carpenter and shipwright who was said to have built the majority of the Plutarch with his own two hands; and even Eirik the Dane, a Swedish man with an identity crisis. It was them and the two dozen other greats that the made the ship run like clockwork, and glide over the seas as if she was floating on air.

I remember as I walked onto that ship how I was greeted by the rest of the crew. Everyone was cold and calculating during work time, but after hours, which is when I joined up, it was nothing but a jolly party, the likes of which could scarce be imagined by the most hedonistic of Romans. They all welcomed me with open arms, especially the big man himself, who despite his station was proud to tussle with the rest of them. The man's might was glorious, he was of average height and build, but his fineries were so immaculate and well sculpted you'd think of him a king before an admiral. His hairy hands were rough from years of hard work, working his way up the ladder to where he was today. It's said of the navy, especially back then, that a man couldn't rise to high station on the sweat of his brow alone, but by the name he carries, well, old admiral Elmwood was the exception to that rule.

Ryan the Lion grew out of the middle class, his father a mason of relatively average standing. Hell, he didn't even have a last name until he was rich enough to provide himself with one. They say he grew up on the shores of Ireland, washed in by a storm as a baby from unknown origin. There his father picked him up and alongside his wife and daughter raised him as his own. That, while some damn fine storytelling is all hogwash unfortunately. In reality, he grew up in an Irish village, like a standard Irish lad, and took to fishing and loved the stories about pirates. That's about all there is to say about his raising, as hard as it is to imagine a man with an average backstory rising to the top of the British navy, I'm afraid it's true.

When I first met him though, the first thing that struck me about him was that he was far from average. He wore spectacles for one thing, a surprise for someone with as good an aim as him, and had a beard that no other man could match, as thick as bear fur and twice as tough. Beneath his admiral's hat lay a short cropped haircut, a style that he himself had a lot of credit in revitalizing. His finery, as stated earlier, was immaculate. With his red coat which he always laid loose, rife with decoration and carvings in the leathers, to his high top boots strapped to the nines with gold and silver buckles, the man's dressing was an art form. It wasn't merely his appearance that awed me though, for his personality was unlike any ship's captain I had ever seen before. If it wasn't for his dress you would've sworn he was another crewman. He was open and kind to everyone, from the lowliest scum scrubber to his first mate. On his ship he knew everyone's name and had a personal relationship with each one of them. Never before had I met such a caring man, even outside of his position. Elmwood cared for his crew like he would his own family, and you could guarantee on his ship that rations were plentiful and that the spirits flowed like a river after work time.

This wasn't the kind of ship where ya needed to drink every day to keep yourself sane, but the kind where you'd drink to celebrate your own good fortune. Don't get me wrong, it was hard work on that tub, harder than I ever had it up to that point, but there was something wonderfully rewarding about the whole thing. Everyday felt like a vacation for men that liked their work, and we were all glad to be there. I would even go days without thinking of my family back home, too enthralled in all the joyous times that were to be had. Even during the firefights we felt comforted. The ship felt invincible, and any significant damage was a rarity to say the least. I don't know if it was the admiral's fine work behind the wheel or the fact that the ship had so many guns that any enemy was more like to get blown out of the water before they even had a chance to react to our presence, but we were the force to be reckoned with out in those waters.

Back home the admiral had a sweetie, he'd never tell us her name, but apparently she was the jewel of Ireland. Each day he'd write to her then seal the letter and store it in this great chest. The lads and I peered in their once, and the trunk despite being the size of a bed was nearly full of wax sealed letters. Of course not all of them were for his gal, a lot of those letters were correspondences that he'd received but never opened from people of all manners, and others were responses that he never sent. This was one of the many mysterious elements behind that great admiral that managed to confound people. He was a complicated man to say the least, far more than he let on, and it was clear he held a dozen secrets in his heart. Others have their theories as to why the admiral never sent those letters at least while I was with him, but I had the feeling that this was a woman he had lost a time afore, and that this was his means of grieving. The only time you'd ever see the man somber was when he came out of that cabin after finishing a composition.

Just when I thought that I was living a life of perfection on board that ship the unthinkable happened, we were to go to battle against Napoleon's hand-picked man o' war. A beast of a ship that stretched its influence all across the northern seas and was looking to stake claim in the channel itself, something that the admiral knew couldn't be allowed, and by the good grace of God, he wasn't going to be the one that allowed it.

      The fight was bloody and hard fought, each side boarding the other's ship and tearing each other to shreds, both by cannons and the arms we carried with us. At the end of it only a handful of us were left, and unfortunately the admiral wasn't among us, or so we thought, lads, or so we thought... What had actually happened was that the admiral fell into the ocean and brought himself to the nearest mass of land, which unfortunately for him was French territory.   After passing out the admiral awoke to the sounds of cannon fire and the whipping of a French flag in the wind, the tri-colour flag of the new republic replacing the fleur de lis of the old monarchy. Luckily for him none of the French had found him, unluckily he seemed to be on the shoreline of a French naval installation. Hungry, thirsty and exhausted the Lion went into survival mode. You can't imagine how quick he did away with that red coat and any British uniform that covered his body. It can be said by the foolish amongst you that this was an act of treachery, but the man knew that the queen needed him back alive more than she needed him wrapped in a red coat at the bottom of the ocean.

      Forced into basically crawling on his knees to avoid detection the poor lad took almost two hours to get out of the installation and back into civilization, if that's what you can call

France that is. He spoke French fluently at least, because of his high rank it was a necessity, but he doubted that he could hide his Irish accent as he spoke it. It was one of the rare times that he felt blessed not to be an Englishman, for as an Irish fellow he could at least tell other that he hated the queen, a common sentiment amongst the Irish at the time, but being a man of high principle he doubted whether he could slander the name of her highness. In France he was a fish out of water to say the least. If he were to be detected it could very well mean his death, and it wouldn't be a pleasant one.

Over the next few days he began to make his way up along the coast, trying to find a charter that could bring him back to his homeland. In the midst of it all he began to use his espionage skills to their fullest. Back in his privateering days where he fought the infamous John Paul Jones of America, he had taken to spying and learning skills of sabotage and subterfuge, skills that he could all put to the test amongst his new found surroundings. Within a day he had a new identity, something that served him well. His design was an Irish separatist, who ran to France to avoid the iron grip of the monarchy. He didn't have a solid reason as to how he would have learned French, so he tried his best to avoid conversation. Near immediately after that he took to grooming himself in the French style, not that his style was particularly English, but you know how the French can be very particular about their style.

21

Lion in the Lurch

I'm looking at you Jacques, bet you can't even understand me. Yeah, you shrug your shoulders.

Anyhow, as you can imagine it wasn't the easiest of tasks to find a ship headed out to England that wasn't in the business of blowing it sky high. There had been a number of occasions where he thought it might be a good idea to head up to Flanders and get out to the island from there, but it wasn't worth the walk, especially considering the Flemish were allied with Napoleon, so it would be almost just as hard to get out through them. His only option was to take a French ship to a neutral land and travel out from there. After a few days' worth of reasoning and planning he managed to hunt down a ship in a town a few miles from where he was located that made trips to Iceland every other month.

After having to wait on foreign soil as a homeless wanderer, slowly burning through the money he had, and working the occasional odd job here and there, the time finally came to leave France for good. He had grown sick and tired of that place and all that it stood for. Now I've been to France and it ain't that bad, but I'm nowhere near as patriotic as a man who goes by the nickname "The Lion", so I don't have much of a frame of reference for his feelings towards the place. Not only that, but you have to remember that at this time the English and the French were mortal enemies, so it would be something akin to having to live under your mother-in-law, if ya need a reference point.

The boat to Iceland, called "The Wanderer", at least translated to English, was no picnic. The grub on board was mostly made up of a variety of fermented fish and whales, though there was a bit of reindeer to go around. The captain of the ship was a grumpy old bastard by the name of Olaf the Cruel. Needless to say the fart's name was well met, and the crew was grinding at the bit within a few days.

Used to running a crew nearly thrice the size of the one he was amongst now, Elmwood found it difficult to be a follower, let alone one under a cruel Icelander, so he began thoughts of staging a mutiny against old Olaf. Now Olaf wasn't a fool, and he caught wind of the situation right quick. One day in the middle of the night Olaf invites the Lion into his cabin, preparing to kill the man, or at the very least throw him overboard. Unfortunately for the grizzly scum, Ryan knew how to fight better than any other man in the crew, and his legend sure wasn't going to end on that old tub if he had anything to say about it.

When he opened that cabin door the first thing he saw was a glint of steel, so he immediately slammed it shut which was followed by the big bang of a gunshot and what could only be an Icelandic swear word. "I'll kill you, Elmwood! That's right, I know who you are. I bet Napoleon will give me a king's bounty for your head," yelled Olaf behind the door.

The Lion booted the captain's door open and shot him straight in the gut before he could even react. "You might have had a chance if you had even a single crewman on your side, ya cold bastard. Now you're just another dead man with a pistol in his hand." Elmwood approached the dying man, who now lay slumped against his back wall in a pool of his own blood, and hauled him up. He started dragging the captain out onto the main deck where the crew lay in wait. "Off ya go, ya vile creature," and with that the Lion threw him off the side of the ship into the freezing waters of the North Sea. The crew hollered in excitement. Though most of the men aboard the ship didn't speak English, he declared himself captain, and the couple that did speak the queen's language translated for the rest of the crew. "We're headed to England, boys. Then you can be off on your merry way."

The Lion gave the crew full reign of the ship, telling them to claim any bounty they so desired, and after they got to England, they could fight amongst themselves for the ship itself, which was directly under Olaf's ownership. Everyone on board knew that the captain, or ex-captain as he now was, didn't have any family, and they'd be damned if anyone missed him. Needless to say the crew were happy with their new captain, who treated them just as well as he would his old crew except this time he didn't care much about the shape of the ship itself, so the work was easy and mild.

By that point in the journey they had already passed England, and were about a day off of the east coast of Scotland, so after checking that his rag tag crew would have the supplies to make it home, he turned the ship around. Five days passed by the time that they reached the shore of England, landing in Sussex. He had already sent word that he was alive and on his way back, a dangerous action were the message to get intercepted, but a danger he was willing to take none the less.

I was lucky enough to be one of the men to meet him once he made landfall, as one of the few men that survived the great battle in the channel. Alongside me included the prime minister of England himself and the duke of Sussex, needless to say I was a bit nervous amongst their company. I remember seeing that old tub roll up over the waves, the harbour ready for its arrival. There he was standing proud on the bow, a smile stretched across his face that you could see from miles away. We all embraced him soon enough, and I'll be damned if it weren't a week 'til he had a ship as big as the Plutarch under his control, and he let that Napoleon know that he wasn't a big fan of the fact that he tore his baby to shreds. Some even say that he was the sole reason behind Britain's naval dominance in the war, for the fury of an Irishman has no bounds.

Matthias Gulgod and the Cult of the Grave Wizard – Strange is as Strange Does

A warning before you dive into this one, it's violent to a grandiose level. You've warned, or perhaps titillated if you're weird enough.

This story was inspired by two very different and very magnificent things, pulp comics of the early 20th century, and a phenomenal human being named Mattie.

Though the intro to the previous story would suggest otherwise there have been very few occasions in my life where I've connected with someone almost immediately and in almost every way. Usually when I meet someone we will get along well enough, after all I'm a relatively personable and pleasant individual, the two of us will have a conversation, and if luck be a lady, the two of us will reconvene at a later date. With Mattie this was not the case, within what must've amounted to only a few seconds I came to realize that I'd met not only a marvelous human being, but a person who basically amounted to being my twin brother, albeit with more than a decade of years between us. That wonderful night when I met Mattie at one of Rod's shows at The Old Crow, and indeed a few other people, who over a few months would come to be some of my closest friends, is perhaps my favourite night of all time.

After our first snippet of a conversation concluded I knew then and there that this man would become a big fixture in my life for many years to come. Perhaps the most humble man I've ever met, who is indeed so humble he'd never admit to such a thing; Mattie is a master in so many elements of life. Above anyone I know, and I know people of all sorts, it is this fine fellow that I could just as easily see as a world renowned philosopher wandering the streets of Ancient Greece, as much as a medieval adventurer braving the high seas, and spreading joy around the known world, like Santa but with a better beard. Here's to you, brother.

I was introduced to pulp fiction through two means, cheesy '80's movies, and H.P. Lovecraft, who I would describe as almost a force of anti-cheese. There's this odd connection between pulp fiction and a significant number of '80's media properties that no one really talks about, but I digress. In truth, I'm not actually that big of a fan of the genre myself, but I am a fan of all the works that came after it. After all it's in those pages that the creation of ridiculous fantasy worlds and superheroes were derived, and although both genres are a bit more serious, and occasionally a lot more serious than their origins, you can't help but to look at that era of work with a sort of nostalgic beauty, even though nearly all of us wouldn't have been alive to see it. There's this certain, almost innate love for cheese that I find a lot of people, have, including myself. Sure, the writing was often abysmal at best, and all the archaic sociological beliefs of that era are on full display, but there's something oddly captivating about the whole idea.

Concerning the story itself, this is one of the few properties that I found myself feeling worried about its reception. Not from a place of nervousness over whether people would enjoy or not, but more because of the hyper violent nature of some of its scenes, it was the first time that I'd ever come across such a sensation. There are other stories that I've written in the past that were just as violent, but it's the fact that I went into the writing of this work with the idea of violence on the forefront that bothered me. It wasn't until about half way into this larger story that I realized it really doesn't matter, it was a tribute to one of the most violent subgenres after all, and violence was the only way to pay proper respect. Another warning, a sort of reward for reading the whole of the intros, this one is a bit droll, a lot of it is just me stating information that came off the top of my head, so it reads a bit "encyclopedic." If you tough it out though, the story does turn into a more traditional style about ¾ of the way through. Either way, I hope you enjoy it!

Matthias Gulgod and the Cult of the Grave Wizard

World War Three was horrible, the worst that the world had even seen. By the time that humanity rose back up to the point of civilization the world had been so radically changed by fallout that a variety of new sciences arose. Most of these sciences, with the warlike mindset that gripped the new world came to be considered forms of magic. Humanity gained a wide range of powers, though only a select few could use them effectively. This story concerns a member of one such groups; highly irradiated humans that were generally referred to as warlocks. Completely opposite to most life that now existed on the world, warlocks lived for an indeterminable amount of time naturally, due to the fact that they almost always died in a state of battle.

War was more common than anything else, from skirmishes between families to the destruction of entire nations, and for a long time warlocks were a key element of this part of society. Only recently has mankind been able to regain control over the Earth, exiling the feral beasts and half-humans through means of conservative yet highly effective weaponry. Warlocks were now obsolete, with the point of their existence being creatures that the higher powers of human society can perform tests on and learn how to enhance their own DNA. At the start of this story, there are a mere 32 warlocks left, the vast majority of which are kept in compounds.

Warlocks were far from the only people that had the ability to access "magic", even at the beginning of this story, though the majority of mankind had returned to its older form of existence, large portions still followed the ways that descended out of the madness of the Great War, that being the development of cults who circled around a specific type of wizard or sorcerer, which were all considered notably different despite their synonymous nature in the English of today. Religion had never been weirder than it was in the days after the war, especially considering how massive some of the cults grew to be, yet lacked organization entirely. Though they were stepping away from it now, in those times the world was nothing more than a complex degree of superstition and misguided faith, if you don't consider the two to be one in the same already.

Drenched in the iridescent blood of the Romanian hog-lizard, Matthias Gulgod continued to tear out the heart of the beast as it lay in its own chest. The sounds of flesh rending from bone were commonplace for the traveler now, once a man of peace now resorting to violence to avenge those he loved. He had travelled day and night for months on end to finally face up against his foe, a 12 foot long beast with the snout and tusks of a warthog and the lithe body of a monstrous iguana, covered in both coarse hair and viscous slime. The Romanian hog-lizard, considered a deity amongst a few recessed cultists in the mountains, had been the cause of his family's destruction a few centuries prior, where he was the only sole survivor. Now coming on his fourth century, in a world where the only course of action for his type was a lifetime of torturous testing or hiding, he gladly chose the latter.

It was a hard fight; the warlock was brought to near death on more than one occasion. This however, was the end for the hog-lizard, the last of its kind, if there had ever been any others. As Matthias yanked with all his might, the hog-lizard tore at his back, shredding through his armour and demolishing his flesh. Both bled more than they ever had before, but only one of them had access to the other's inner organs. If one were to listen closely, over the screams of both man and beast they could hear the cracking rib cage of the hog-lizard as the warlock tried his best to keep it pried open, using his elbows and the strength of his biceps to resist the thousand kilos of pressure bearing down on him from the creature's healing factor. With all of the beast's resistance though, a final monstrous seizure of power led to Matthias tearing the half ton heart out of the beast and throwing it to the far end of the cave.

In a final surge of life the hog-lizard flipped around and attempted to lunge for its heart. Knowing that there was a good chance that the heart would still be active for a couple of seconds, and thus able to reattach itself if brought in close enough proximity to the creature, Matthias grabbed the beast's tale and hauled it as hard as he could towards himself. There wasn't much strength left in the old warlock, but it proved to be enough as the beast slumped on the floor dead with one final gasp of air.

Matthias, emotionally and physically exhausted, not to mention bleeding to death, fell to the ground in a pile of torn flesh and cloak and prepared for his own demise. Knowing full well that he would never wake again, the Warlock took one final rest on that cave floor, content with life and the vengeance he wrought on the creature that terrorized him and his family all those years ago. He could still to that day remember the screams of his beloved as she was torn in two by the beast, and the cry for help uttered by his child, his last words before being consumed alive. Now though, in his mind he heard their thanks and contentment as they reveled over his victory, and he was glad to be reunited with them soon enough.

The sounds of heavy breathing and chanting from far away corridors woke him up. Unable to move anything other than his head he looked down at his body, which lay paler than he remember and covered in the sutures of repaired wounds and sewn together body parts. His arms, he could see, were strung high on either side of him; his legs strung low, putting his body in a spread eagle position. He was not entirely naked, a cloth draping covered in blood and other unidentified ichors covered his genitalia, which was actually something that annoyed him quite a bit because he had the sinking feeling that they were severed during his fight in Romania.

Being nearly four hundred years old this certainly wasn't the first time he'd been captured, not even the first time that it happened when he assumed death was in his reach. After all, warlocks had the unfortunate power of managing to avoid death through what seemed to the outsider like luck alone. He had two assumptions for who captured him, but both of them didn't add up. Sure it could have been Kerlov the mountain Druid, the two had hated each other ever since Kerlov tried to sacrifice Matthias to the bear god and the warlock ignited his beard with ghost fire. Why would Kerlov fix his wounds though? There was the possibility that his captor was Heinrich the Purple, another warlock who was a big fan of selling his own kind to the imperials for testing, but he was nowhere near there, and as far as Matthias knew, he had no knowledge of teleportation. Standing there pinned to what could only be described as a giant, yet highly ornate "X", Matthias was out of ideas as to who could've captured him and for what reason. He also began to think of the pale pigment that spread across his once tanned skin. "I better not be undead you grimy fucks, that's the last thing I need," he whispered to himself, and then yelled with all the might of his lungs.

Being a warlock Matthias unbound himself within a couple minutes, surprised to see there was no magic on the wire that tied him down. After quickly checking to see his genitalia intact, he moved on. Looking around the room that he was in, a reinforced cave or hole in the ground based on the fact that the walls were made of dirt, he noticed a large locked chest in the far corner. Matthias couldn't stand, his muscles atrophied from being hung up for an indeterminable amount of time. Crawling his way to the far corner, word of unlocking sitting readily on his lips, Matthias took notice of how none of his wounds were opening. This showed that he was either very lucky, or unlucky depending on how you looked at it. Sure, he wouldn't have to worry about infection down here, but it also meant that he had been down in this hole for at least a few weeks, though probably more. Whoever had been keeping him down here couldn't be too far away, because someone had been keeping him fed and hydrated. He had to move with haste, but that option wasn't exactly in the cards. He also couldn't help but regret yelling a few moments earlier, the old warlock was in no shape to fight.

After crawling in the pain of muscle atrophy for what felt like hours, but couldn't have amounted to more than just a few minutes, the warlock reached the chest and heaved it open through the assistance of his sorcery. As he guessed, inside of the chest he found his belongings, including his armour that had been painstakingly repaired to the level that it hadn't looked in years. Even all the runestones that the Norwegian seithmann Eirikr the Grey had installed were now at full power, something only a shaman could do, or at the very least a very powerful life wizard.

Hearing footsteps coming from afar, Matthias pulled himself into the chest, which luckily had enough room to fit him and his belongings. From here his magic still worked despite the lack of oxygen, so he was able to return the chest to its original locked position.

"By the cathar's beast! He's gone, the warlock has disappeared!"

They were speaking English, a language that Matthias hadn't hear fluently spoken in a couple of decades at least, ever since most of England was annihilated after the fall of the Gravekin, their primary source of magic dwellers. The mention of the beast of cathar was another revealing hint, it proved almost without question that these folk were under the rule of a cathartic, meaning they were probably a shore based cult with a life wizard at their head.

After listening to their continued shouting and rumbling throughout the room, including a few feeble attempts to open the chest, the warlock could finally hear them leaving the room.

Matthias Gulgod and the Cult of the Grave Wizard

As soon as no one could be heard even with the warlock's projected hearing, the lid of the chest flung open revealing a figure floating above the chest covered in a series of black patchwork cloaks and a skull painted onto his face. A grave wizard, this was a gods damned grave wizard cult.

Assuming it would be seconds until his skeleton started to dissolve beneath his skin, Matthias hastily searched through the belongings beneath him for something that could reverse the effects. Finding nothing, Matthias prepared his mind for the most painful fate a man could be subjected to. Taking a deep breath and accepting his situation, the warlock was wonderfully surprised when the apparition dissipated right in front of his eyes. Grave wizards were one in a million when England was still around, but now that the Gravekin were no longer, aside from, he supposed, this group, Matthias had a feeling he had just met eye to eye with the world's last living grave wizard.

The danger of the grave wizards was one of the primary reasons behind the destruction of England, which was often seen as the haven for life wizards. Grave wizards, though specializing in the nature of death, still used a form of life magic. Life wizards are far from a rarity nowadays, and can be found in large numbers nearly everywhere of earth, often as a Mage alternative to doctors. Those with a significant amount of wisdom have declared life magic the easiest to learn, but the hardest to master. It was above the step of being a master that a grave wizard could be developed though, it took a wide variety of specific circumstances with the easiest being one of the best life wizards in existence.

Before that point Matthias had actually met a grave wizard. It was a nameless creature, covered in rotting flesh, with the majority of its body just made up of exposed bone, aside from its face which was painted in the style of the Gravekin, a skull which highlighted its facial features. That was the day that he had lost his family, the day that the hog-lizard devoured his family whole and wiped out nearly half of the warlock population. It wasn't until today that he had the notion that the two might have been connected.

Matthias met the grave wizard that day on the field of battle. As a young warlock Matthias worked for the government of Hungary to clean up battlefields and try his best to save any maimed soldiers, or give them a pleasant death. Gravekin weren't a rarity after a battle in those times, usually feeding on the souls of the deceased, but that time there were no Gravekin, just that horrid monster of a wizard. He had heard enough about the nature of grave wizards to know that he ought to run, but he was frozen, possibly by magic influence, but more than likely it was just the power of curiosity.

The grave wizard hadn't seen him yet, as it was facing the other direction, it raised its arms and a bunch of ooze started to leave all the corpses on the field and slide towards the wizard who absorbed the substance through its hands. At the time the warlock had no idea what the substance was, but a few centuries of experience gives one a bit of knowledge, so he had now come to recognize the abominable substance as concentrated soul. Usually when a Gravekin feeds on the soul of the deceased it only requires a small amount, not even enough to disturb the rest of the afflicted. Concentrated soul however, was the entirety of that being's existence, pulled not only from what remained of its corpse, but also the elements that had already passed on to the other side. It was a horrific thing to be subjected to, and it was apparently only an ability that grave wizards could use.

There wasn't much knowledge on grave wizards aside from the destructive abilities that they possessed. Since theirs was still a school of life magic, it was likely that they had vast powers of restoration, but never has anyone recorded one of the creatures doing something that benefitted anything aside from themselves. The majority of information about the species came from the recording of Robby Tooley, a Gravekin that left the order prior to even the birth of Matthias Gulgod. Since the passage was so ancient, about an almost legendary creature, in a language that no longer existed, the ideas portrayed in the text were never properly translated, not to mention that it was a pretty unpopular book in its time. Matthias had no problem with reading it though, it came from his time so he could understand the dialects used, he spoke fluent English, and he was well aware of the importance of knowing about grave wizards, at least before they were all but wiped off the Earth.

According to the work, it was through the grave wizards that Gravekin were first created, a mixture of a normal human DNA and the highly irradiated cells of the grave wizard. Due to this, Gravekin often found themselves flocking to the creatures. There was no actual benefit to being around a grave wizard because they didn't care for the Gravekin in the slightest, or even enhance their abilities through the radiation that they gave off. The strangest thing that grave wizards did with Gravekin was the fact that they did nothing at all. They were the only humans that they wouldn't actively kill, in fact they seemed to ignore them entirely. According to Tooley, grave wizards were big fans of torture, getting not pleasure from sadism, but more life force from creating fear and anguish. In fact, Tooley tells us that grave wizards not only don't speak, but don't seem to engage in any actions that would be necessary for all other forms of sentient life, aside from the consumption of soul forces.

When it comes to the work on the attack powers of a grave wizard the primary text that everyone refers to is Alphagia Scrotus' recount of the war on England in the 29th century, another rare and understated find. Matthias had actually met Scrotus, a regular human, because they had done a

Matthias Gulgod and the Cult of the Grave Wizard

few studies together in his days as a scholar. He was an interesting man to say the least, albeit a bit confrontational, neither of which showed in his writing which was duller than a rubber mallet. In the recount Scrotus talks of the stories he heard from soldiers, a few of which revolve around the rare sighting of a grave wizard. Surprisingly given the degree of their powers grave wizards were susceptible to ballistic fire, even though they were very hard to hit due to their ability of dissolution and teleportation. Scrotus recounts the tale of a sole survivor of a battle against Gravekin in which a grave wizard wiped out the whole of a platoon with a single surge of magic, dissolving their skin and causing them to bleed out if they didn't commit suicide because of the pain. In another instance a grave wizard dissolved a soldier's bones inside his body, followed by the liquid bone secreting out his skin, which is often cited as the most painful death imaginable by man. The memoirs also talk of the grave wizards' abilities to raise Gravekin from the dead for a few minutes to defend the wizard. There are a few errors in the text though. For one, Scrotus talks about how the grave wizards will risk their own lives to save Gravekin, a "fact" that he himself made up, while the very opposite is true. The only time a grave wizard will kill one of its cultist is if it's dying, absorbing their soul while they're still alive to prolong its own life.

Ever since that fateful war it was concluded by all magical societies that the grave wizards had been wiped out entirely, and that the Gravekin were only alive in fleeting pockets amongst the scarred landscape of their once proud homes. Where ever Matthias was now, it was obvious that the place had grown quite developed. Intricate English art and carvings covered the walls and decorated the furniture. Steel bearings and masonry helped to keep things together. There was no way that this was a new installation, but probably one made around the war itself, though probably right after. This realization told Matthias two things, he was in England, meaning he'd travelled across almost all of Europe, and that the Gravekin were still around.

Knowing the nature of grave wizards, the warlock knew that it hadn't informed the cultists of his whereabouts, so he took the opportunity to do as much escaping as he could. Getting enough balance to pull himself out the chest, Matthias made his way to the hallway entrance, clearly marked by containment glyphs. The warlock was legitimately insulted that these cultists thought that they could contain him with such abysmal magic. Matthias sliced open his hand with the knife that he retrieved from chest, and drew a portal on the invisible wall that sat in front of him, then crawled through it. A simple enough counter glyph, but the wound was going to be annoying.

As he feebly tried again and again to stand up, he quickly came to the realization that this wasn't just atrophy, and took a closer look at his legs. It seemed that the cultists had drilled holes in his Achilles' tendons. Clearly this group had never dealt with a warlock before, and upon realizing this to be the case, Matthias used what blood remained on his wound to repair the sinew, giving him the ability to painfully wander his way to safety. Now that he could actually stand, the warlock decided he should go back for his belongings before moving forward at all, thinking that he might need more than a simple knife. When he returned to his impromptu jail cell, Matthias found that the chest had been locked once again. At first he just thought that he must have forgot the fact that he locked it to cover his tracks, but there was no magic to this lock, it was a whole new padlock of an entirely physical origin. A teleporter with physicality must have done this, unless someone was in the room the entire time, an unlikely occurrence given the warlock's enhanced senses. This wasn't the work of the grave wizard, both because it wouldn't have cared enough, and the beings tended not to do well with physicality, lacking any sufficient dexterity due to their rotting flesh. A teleporter was another significant hurdle that the warlock would have to overcome before he could leave. Teleportation was a very difficult magic to learn, and even in Matthias' four centuries of life he had only conjured enough ability to travel a couple of feet, and it would wipe him out for a few hours, turning him nearly comatose. It was often enough to save him in a dire situation though.

Within seconds the lock was off once more and the warlock grabbed all his belongings, equipping as much as he felt lucky enough to have the time to take. Putting on clothing proved to be an arduous task due the damage inflicted by the atrophy, but he managed to equip his entire wardrobe over the course of five minutes. It seemed that the Gravekin didn't rummage through his clothing, as most of the pockets still contained the belongings that were in them at the time of his battle with the hog-lizard. Not only that, but some of them were repaired, including his cloak, which must have been washed thoroughly in order to get what could only be pints and pints of blood from both himself and the beast that he slew. The objects that weren't still in the place that he'd left them were merely situated amongst the bottom of the trunk after they had innocently tumbled out. He did however notice the absence of two glass bottles, both of which seemed to broken due to the occasional glass remnant or two he'd find amidst the pile.

All of his weaponry was there also, for though he never really found a need to use much of it, they could always be used in a tight squeeze, especially the guns. The weapon that any warlock used most often was their mind followed closely by a sacrificial dagger used to convene blood magic, utilizing the radioactive material set deep in their tissue. For Matthias the use of weapons was always a sign of weakness, a certain degree of finesse was involved, sure, and the engineering behind a number of them was magnificent. To the warlock a gun was nothing compared the human mind though, and any assistance needed in that factor was an outrage, though his critics have often said that such a claim was far easier to make with the force of magic on one's side.

With his belongings now in tow the warlock headed on, making sure to be quite wary of his surroundings. There was little more dangerous than the unknown to a warlock. Anything that could hide itself from other's senses was the warlock's ultimate enemy, and there were at least two such beings in this cavern. An adept teleporter tended to have control over the entirety of their molecular structure, using a type of hex magic known as disintegration or advanced pyromancy, they could hide everything from their appearance to their smell, with their only noticeable factor being their footfalls and that uneasy feeling that one gets when someone's looking at them. The grave wizard on the other hand was completely hidden, in truth one could have been floating right behind Matthias and he wouldn't be able to tell. It certainly didn't help that they had highly enhanced reaction time, so they could easily disappear out of sight as fast as they could reappear to reap souls.

The hallway outside of the room that Matthias was contained in was quite short, with only three doors attached to it, not including the open portal that connected to the room that the warlock awoke in. From what he could tell, two of the rooms were storage, full of mundane items and the third led to a larger room, at least from what he could sense.

Unlocking the closest storage room he proved himself correct, the only notable items being a few flasks filled to the brim with regenerative poultices and other healing potables. Normally Matthias would simply leave the items, a sort of courtesy for his captors leaving his own belongings alone, but on this occasion the warlock knew that he could use all the help that he could get to aid his journey. The second storage room however was much more promising, aside from some regular cleaning equipment, the closet contained a horde of grave goods, all arranged in sealed jars and cans. With objects such as; bones, jewelry, organs and really anything else one could find on a dead body, it showed Matthias that this group was still very much active, and that they had developed the magic to keep soul items for later that they could feast on, an impressive group to say the least. It became evident to the wizard by this point that the group had allowed him to escape. They were far too knowledgeable in all others ways than to make such feeble trappings for a warlock of Matthias' ability; for some reason they were trying to trick him into underestimating them, but he wasn't sure as to why.

When approaching the third door Matthias knew that he had to be cautious. There was clearly something or someone inside there, but he couldn't tell if it was human or beast.

Matthias Gulgod and the Cult of the Grave Wizard

Whatever it was, it was large and bipedal. Uttering magic to silence his movements the warlock threw the door open and didn't generate a single sound. Inside he was happy to see that the creature that awaited him was none more than a blind martyr, a humanoid mole beast, that had merely got itself trapped in the underpinnings of the burrow. Aside from looking horrendous these creatures were utterly harmless, only capable of eating the bacteria in dirt. It was lost, but it's hole lay only 30 feet to its left, so the warlock had no doubt it would find its way home without his assistance, and it wasn't worth accidentally alarming some of the Gravekin to give the noble beast any assistance in the matter.

Running across the floor silently the warlock accessed the nearest empty room, going off his senses. Another hallway, though this time much longer, and with many more doors. It seemed to be the Gravekin barracks, another empty lead to the outside world.

"Warlock." A young woman came out of the nearest room to his left. "We've been waiting for you for quite some time. There's no need to fear for your life this is a peaceful place, after all we saved you from certain death three months past."

"Three months, is that how long it's been? I suppose that fits the timeline I've constructed for myself. What could you Gravekin want from me? I am old, tired and long prepared for death. I will take my life quicker than I'd let you sell me to the imperial forces. I will be no one's guinea pig."

"Worry not, brave scholar, we have no interest in you as a warlock, but as a man of letters. As I'm sure you've noted, a grave wizard lives amongst us, it is in fact the last grave wizard in existence. Help us in recording his memoirs and we will let you go even if your attempt is futile. Otherwise we will still leave you be, but you will die a painful death of starvation soon enough."

"Why keep me locked in such a state though? An invisible wall, a locked chest, was it some sort of fail-safe in case I wasn't who you thought I was?"

"Ah, well, no. That was simply the machinations of some of our members who are quite a bit lower down the totem pole. A practice session gone awry if you will. Then, as we were going to take it down, we figured it might be good practice for you, so we drilled holes in your tendons for a little more difficulty. A lot of it came out of boredom, a bit out of spite. Not all of us have had the best times with warlocks in the past." Through the look that cultist gave the warlock, he could tell that she wasn't one of them. She also doubted that this was the teleporter, but merely some degree of shaman, in short, no one to be afraid of.

"Well, to be honest it has been quite a long time since I've done any scholarly work. Perhaps this would lead to a certain degree of personal satisfaction. I'm assuming you're not going to give me any sort of compensation for this are you? That I'm just expected to complete the task and that my freedom is enough of an incentive."

"Oh, we hadn't expected you to be so casual about the whole thing, but yes we do have some funds to pay you with, plus free room, board and meals. We have quite the commune down here. Who knows, you may even find it an enjoyable experience in the end."

"Hmm, yes, I'm sure, nothing greater than being held captive to deal with a homicidal monster on a daily basis." It could be expected that a Gravekin would be offended by such words, though luckily sarcasm tended to escape them.

Matthias observed his surroundings as the Gravekin discussed his living quarters, and what would be expected. He actively ignored it, knowing that he would stay and do what he wanted and that the only person that had the capability to stop him was the grave wizard itself, which wouldn't care in the slightest. Looking around he noticed that there were no other cultists in the near vicinity, in fact there wasn't anyone at all nearby aside from the blind martyr.

"So, where is everybody and why aren't you with them?"

"They're at the sound hall, someone swore that they saw the grave wizard there, and they're going to do their prayers. I don't need to hunt down the great one, for I'm his handler and he actively seeks me out, which is why the two of us will be working closely together. Just to let you know, I have no problem with warlocks. I find your kind fascinating." This was no ordinary Gravekin, she lacked the glassy eyes and the absence of any sort of wonder. Matthias doubted whether she was a Gravekin at all, but someone more akin to an outsider cultist, one who dissuades the temptation of a cult's abilities and is just truly interested in the priorities and beliefs in the cult. Since Gravekin had abilities in sorcery this was a rarity among their kind, even at their height, she was a scholar after Matthias' own heart.

Back in a day when warlocks were in higher standing Matthias accidentally created his own cult. It was during his days of wandering the feral lands. There was a compound filled with small, orphaned children, hungry from years of being alone and foraging without the appropriate skills that they required to live a fulfilled life. Being a good man back in those days, Matthias took a few of the children under his wing, teaching those skills of survival and how to deal with the harsh natural conditions of their homeland. Soon enough more joined, and while magic was rarely used in his aid of others, people came to see him as some sort of deity who could heal the sick and cure all ailments known to man. Before long it was much more than a group of orphaned children, but all the towns in the

Matthias Gulgod and the Cult of the Grave Wizard

surrounding area. While there were a sensible few, usually those that started following him early, the majority of the people there were fanatic to say the least. One night, after everyone had fallen asleep because Matthias had given them strict orders to lie in bed all night and leave for no reason until the morning, he snuck away in the shadow of night, using as many speed incantations as he could muster, causing his body to nearly give way under all the g-forces. Due to this unfortunate age in his history he almost sympathized with the grave wizard, if they weren't so brutally vicious of course.

"Alright, let's say I work with you and your cult. What kind of promise do you have that this grave wizard won't rend my flesh from my bones? I've dealt with their kind in the past, and they don't tend to be the friendliest bunch, no matter how much your kind adores them."

"To be honest, we can't really guarantee anything, otherwise we'd just put up a job posting. You were kidnapped for a reason. You're one of the few people on Earth who is qualified for the position, and once we found you unconscious and bleeding out, we'd figured that you would have even more incentive to help us, what with us saving your life and all. Yes, though, in conclusion there really is no safe guard that the wizard doesn't kill you, though he does know why you're here, so that will probably prove worthwhile to your advantage."

50

"Fair enough, a death is a death anyhow, I've had bones torn out of me before, and I know pain well enough."

"So, you'll do it?!" The young cultist's smile could light up a room.

"Yes, I'll do it. I'm going to sleep where I want and I'll put my hat down wherever I wish, I'm not going to be some prisoner. I will have full access to each room and all of the facilities, and if I feel my life is in danger I am well within my right to carry out whatever actions I deem necessary. Agreed?"

Matthias stuck out his hand, but was soon embraced by the cultist. "You won't regret being alive to do this, warlock! Thank you, thank you! Now let me give you a full tour of the facilities that lie before you.

"To start off with, we're somewhere deep below the farthest south-eastern corner of England, the least contaminated part of all of Britain. As far as we know there aren't any other Gravekin, or really anyone else for that matter in this part of the world. Like I told you before, our leader is almost with all certainty the last grave wizard on this planet. Therefore you can imagine the safety of this area."

The young cultist whose name was revealed to be Marill was extremely bright, and the tour that she gave Matthias was succinct and highly informative of exactly the circumstances that would affect him the most. Though he hid his feelings, Matthias was actually quite amazed at the complex that he found himself in. It was very well-built, and even quite decorated in a traditional medieval Gothic style. The more common rooms, despite being underground, had great vaulted ceilings, some measuring a good 50 meters in height. The studies, which seemed rarely used, were numerous, and the magical properties were still potent in all of them. Matthias came to the conclusion that this place was far older than the cultist was letting him know. This must have been created at least a couple of decades prior to the war on England, due to the amount of wealth put into this place. The decorations were also quite different from what he'd seen in Gravekin establishments a long time ago. Despite the difference in décor a lot of what he saw on the tour reminded him of his old campaigns in England.

Much like every Gravekin den he'd seen, there was a large central flagellation chamber, where the members of the cult would come to wound themselves in the name of repentance. It was a technique adapted from the Middle Ages, but a bit more adapted to the technology available. Instead of scoring themselves with whips and flaying instruments, which they believed damaged the consecrated nature of the hall, the group took to bloodless techniques such as electrocution or small scale immolation. They would often work in pairs, torturing one another in order to commit to their religious beliefs to the utmost extent.

From his own research into the subject, Matthias had read that the reason behind the flagellation chamber being the largest is that it was the most likely location for the grave wizard to inspect, thus providing him with more glory and majesty. This was one of the facts that confused Matthias as to his purpose amongst the group. Clearly they desired for him to chronicle the grave wizard as a creature to better understand its purpose and desires, yet at the same time, with centuries of existence one could assume that they had gathered enough evidence over the years on the creatures that the recordings of a single scholar surely wouldn't be enough to satisfy. There was something else afoot in all this, and until he could find out what it was for himself, he would keep his suspicions to himself.

With the tour concluded Matthias retired to a room that he decided to make his own. It was small, and had previously been used for storage. He asked for a straw bed, but got a foam mattress in its stead. It was an odd feeling, that level of comfort. He also managed to snag himself a mirror, it was likely that they would have given him one if he just asked, but he didn't want to get too comfortable with their hospitality.

In that mirror as he looked over his corpse, he felt along all the scars that lay across his body. Before the battle with the hog-lizard he was far from the prettiest of men, with at least a couple dozen of scars, but now he was utterly covered in them.

Matthias Gulgod and the Cult of the Grave Wizard

They must have covered a good 80% of his flesh. Some of the scar tissue hadn't healed as properly as he would've liked, leading to deep canyons in his flesh. He couldn't help but to compare himself to the grave wizard that he was supposed to be looking after.

"Ah, so you're the teleporter that's been hiding in the shadows," said Matthias as he saw a young man appear out of thin air with a blast of flame. It was pyromancy, the kind that preys on the energy of living beings, the fires in their soul, a very dangerous and difficult skill to master. Knowing pyromancy, it was also unlikely that the man that stood behind him was as young as he appeared, gathering the souls of living beings tended to leave your own pretty well-nourished. Pyromancers and Gravekin worked together quite often in the past, so it wasn't the biggest surprise to see one in this place.

"My name is Nickolaj," the man spoke in Romanian. "I am the one that saved you from the beast's lair. You know, my father once prayed under that beast in a time long past, so you could say you've done my family quite the injustice. Then again, I despise the entirety of my family, so if anything I'm pleased."

"Nice to meet you, Nickolaj, it's hard to find another person skilled in a variety of magic these days, even harder to find those who would still call it as such. From one old timer to another, why are you working for these Gravekin?"

The Romanian flame artist laughed, "Well, from one old man to another, I have to say that I simply love their vigor. Did you know that these are the very last Gravekin on Earth? There's only about 800 of them in total, 95% of which must be in this very complex. It's almost as if I'm redeeming myself from a past of hunting them down. A rogue pyromancer is no longer rogue when the people that made him such become the norm.

"You know, Gulgod, we have actually met a few times, during the wars on these very plains. You were still a scholar mostly at that point, although when you used your skills in war it was always as if one was watching a master artist paint on a canvas. I have no recollection of what my name was back then, I'm sure you'll forgive me for such. The magics have their effect on the brain after all, as I'm sure you know."

"The only way I ever remembered is because I had it tattooed on my arm, back before the scars; right under this one here actually, if I recall. Those were good times, my fellow, when people like us were actually respected instead of vilified. Sure, we were little more than weapons to use, but at least we had a sense of purpose, direction even."

"Ah, I'm afraid that I don't share the same sentiment, though I certainly see where you're coming from. I was simply always about working against the grain, being a rebel no matter the cost. That was easy enough to get in those days as it is now. After all, I was a terrible soldier. I must have gotten caught a good dozen times before I called it quits. They always think us teleporters are so naturally skilled in espionage, but I'm afraid that I'm very much the antithesis of that argument."

The two old men had a few more laughs in them before the conversation turned to business. It seems that they had been in a lot of the same places at the same time. Nickolaj proved good company at least. It had been a long time since Matthias spoke at length to another person, especially one with a situation similar to his own.

"Ah, you're a good man Matthias, better than I remembered even. It seems time has not made you too grouchy for a good conversation. Well, I suppose it's time that we got down to business.

"As you may have guessed by now, I was the one that gave your name to the group. They found you, tracked you down and when the time was right sent me to gather you. I know you're a bright man and you've come to the conclusion that these people haven't brought you here to use your abilities as a scholar, so you might as well hear the truth from me.

"You're a smart man, I'm sure you know that the grave wizard here is the last in the world. What you might not have realized is that the thing is dying, slowly but clearly dying. As the foremost master on grave wizards the cultists here and I have surmised that it has little more than a couple years left. They're mysterious beings, but there are some truths about them that people like us can't help to notice. The creature is gaining weight and skin. When a wizard, warlock or sorcerer becomes a grave wizard, they lose all their skin and are basically just a mass of bone with a face, kept alive via magic alone. As their magic begins to run out they start building organs to keep up with their functions."

"I'll do it."

"Excuse me?"

"Oh, come on don't get coy with me now. I said I'll be your next grave wizard, teach me how. You do know how, don't you?"

"Well, I mean yes, but how'd you know? Ah, I knew you were the right man for the job! I saw it in your eyes back then; the guilt as you flattened those Gravekin and tore them limb from limb using your life magic. The books on you even say that you were once considered the greatest master of life magic in the world, but you gave it up."

"Books on me? There was only the three ever printed, you must really be quite the scholar. Yes though, maybe it's the guilt, maybe it's because I lack purpose, but I'm done with this life I'm leading. I'll be your next grave wizard."

To be continued next time in...

Matthias Gulgod and the Change of Aeons

Matthias Gulgod and the Cult of the Grave Wizard

The Great North – In the Heart of Confusion

This is one of those stories where you really have no clue what you're going to turn it into when it begins, and by the end, you're still not entirely sure what you've created. I started off the story with the possibility that I'd turn it into a survival story with comedy elements, then I went into basically a full comedy, and by the end I suppose it was something akin to a small spiritual journey. As it goes with most stories that are so sporadic, I was highly tempted to throw this one by the wayside, and simply call it a lost amount of words. Eventually I came to the realization that perhaps the lack of a proper compass is something akin to an actual traumatic situation. After all this is a story about a person, much like me, who both can't handle stress nor has any idea of what to do in a survival situation. There's a great deal of misplays in this story, but at the same time it's relatively short, and I actually found myself finding the end result quite interesting, simply due to the lack of meaning.

If this spin hasn't convinced you of the purpose for me to put this story in the collection, then I suppose you can just take it as an example of my poor writing. Perhaps it's a good thing to have samples from all degrees of my possible abilities.

Though this may not be everyone's favourite story, it is the one most inspired by my transformation into a much more social lifestyle. In many ways I had my own sort of spiritual awakening when I came out of my proverbial shell, and though I'm not fully there yet, there was a couple of moments that caused a big revelation leading to my edging closer to a fully-fledged, socially capable human being. In a lot of ways what transpires in this book reminds me of my own metamorphosis, although what happened to me was far less dramatic.

The Great North

As Greg exhaled his breath quickly turned to a white puff and drifted off with the wind. He had always imagined the Great North as some sort of magical wonderland, but the truth was much more intense than he had imagined.

"Not a lot to see here, eh?"

"Nope."

"No trees or anything?"

"Nope."

"How do you guys survive out here?"

"Fish. Imports."

"But, what do you do for fun?"

His guide looked over to him, his face completely covered. Greg could only imagine the amount of hate and anger emanating from that stare. "Fish. Go." The lumbering man began to plod forward, his large flat shoes leaving tennis racket sized impressions in the snow. Greg followed close behind, although his pace was less reliable.

"Is the camp nearby? Or, not the camp, the outpost. Yeah, is the outpost nearby?"

"Yes," the guide threw his arm forward in the direction of a faint yellow glow in the distance.

Within a few minutes the outpost was completely visible. The guide was outpacing Greg significantly, and before

The Great North

Greg realized he found himself quite behind. In a feeble attempt to catch up he started to jog, but he had been warned that sweating was an all too grim reality when wearing what seemed to be fifty pounds in thermal clothing. Greg called out to his companion. Hearing the call the guide turned around, stopped moving and stood there.

Filled with embarrassment Greg began to jog once again, following the guide's footsteps. He came to a point along his guide's trail where a wide turn was made which returned to the straight path a few meters past. Thinking this would make a fine shortcut, Greg decided to cut across the turn.

As soon as he took a step off the guide's trail he found himself falling, wedged between two icy walls in a small ravine that had been covered up by a thin layer of hardened snow. Greg began to scream.

Up above Greg could hear the approaching steps of the guide, sticking to the same plodding pace he had grown so used to over the past few hours.

"Follow the path," the guide looked down into the crevice, and in view of Greg opened his fur backpack, then proceeded to throw down some food. "Follow the path. Eat. Sleep. Be back soon."

As the food fell down on him, Greg stopped his screaming. "What is this?! Don't you have a rope or something?! Save me!"

"Be back soon. Morning, maybe sooner," with that the guide left Greg's view and began to walk away.

Greg started screaming again, and crying, mostly crying.

As he sat in that hole, screaming and crying, his head filled with thoughts of anger, remorse and confusion. He thought about his family back home, how they'd react once they hear he died. He thought about his wife and daughter, waiting for him in the outpost. Mostly though, he thought about the guide. *Morning, maybe sooner*. The man could barely speak a word of English, but there are so many things Greg should have asked him. Should I sleep now? Do you think I'll starve to death? What will you say to my family? Deep down Greg knew it didn't matter, the guide would have just shrugged, grunted, but maybe he would have said, "Nope," and my God that would be all the reassurance he'd need. In fact, Greg started to think, I bet he would have said no, I bet he's already on his way back. Unfortunately for Greg it had been mere minutes since he'd left so that wasn't a possibility in the slightest, but it's good he got his spirits up.

An hour passed, nothing had happened. Greg's tears had left trails of ice all over his face.

Another hour passed, nothing had happened. Greg began to look through the food the guide had thrown down. It was all fish.

The Great North

A third hour passed, nothing had happened. Greg began to move along the ravine, before quickly finding himself at the edge of it. He then started to move in the other direction. The ravine proved to be no more than ten meters long, but it was enough to walk around in.

He decided to try the fish, it was salted. Yeah, it was definitely salted. There's nothing like the taste of partially rotting, ridiculously salty fish to raise the spirits. As he began to look through the food the whale blubber caught his attention. It's supposed to be a delicacy, right? Greg had eaten around the world, well in Los Angeles, at the finest five star restaurants. He knew delicacies, and how they had varying degrees of taste quality. Well, polarizing might be a better word, either tasty beyond belief, or rancid to a degree that he had previously thought impossible for something edible.

Maybe, he began to think to himself; just maybe he could have prepared more for this journey. I mean, of course he knew it was going to be cold; he was all bundled up to the nines, so he probably wouldn't freeze to death. He could have done more survival research though. Shouldn't he know how to deal with this exact situation?

It was strange how he'd get bursts of confidence and optimism, and then overbearing feelings of dread and impending doom. He'd go one minute thinking that the guide was a master at this sort of thing, so he'd be perfectly fine and the next minute he came to the frightening realization that it was possible that the canyon would soon cave in and crush his innards. This was so unlikely that it was almost impossible, but the thought occurred to him none the less.

At one point Greg began to recall the story of that forest ranger that got hit by lightning more times than you can count on one hand. What if a storm began to brew? I mean sure, he was underground in a tight ravine, and the insulated suit that he wore would almost entirely negate the electricity, but what if it struck him in the face?!

Within a couple of hours Greg found himself hungry once more. The salt fish was apparently less filling than he'd assumed. As he was looking through his pack for more fish he found one of those weird space blankets tucked away in the corner. He immediately wrapped it around himself, and felt an odd sense of security. He was already plenty warm, in fact the ravine was quite cozy, so the blanket wasn't necessary. Within a couple of minutes he was almost hot, something that Greg felt perfectly fine with.

Greg's face, still remarkably uncovered, started to tighten. His skin had grown a dense film of sweaty ice on it. He had been warned about sweating, in fact he had thought about the possibility a few times, but for some indescribable reason brought about by the panic of an emergency situation he had forgotten all about it. In desperation Greg threw off the blanket, and his coat, and his vest. Now he was in a long shirt, still warm, and still drenched in sweat. He began to try to warm his face once it became difficult to manipulate his eye lids. Soon enough the sweaty ice began to melt off and his face, now pleasantly warm was safer from the elements.

Another problem had developed though. His long sleeve sweater had his sweat soaked into it and had also started to freeze, something that he failed to notice as he sat as still as possible in fear that he would generate more sweat. On top of that he was starting to get cold. Due to his now limited mobility it took him a good five minutes to get his coat back on, in which time the sweat that covered his interior layers had caused the clothes to stick his body resulting in a burning feeling.

As a man who'd lived in the south-western United States his whole life, this was the first time in his life in which he'd felt the ill effects of cold aside from the simple difference in temperature. He had not been prepared for such a feeling, and found himself petrified when the sensation hit him; soon enough though, he mustered the courage to do up his coat. He was proud of himself, and at the same time a little embarrassed when he realized it couldn't possibly be real heat, but a sensation of the cold being abrasive against his flesh, much like when it's really windy.

After a good half hour of simply walking around, and finally covering up his face, the situation rectified itself, he was now comfortably warm, and hopefully not sweaty enough for any more nonsense to occur. As a professional researcher, Greg couldn't help but see this event as a learning experience, yet at the same time he cried to the high heavens for his misfortune.

By nature Greg was not a solitary man. He was very sociable, people had even commented on his sociability, or so he misremembered, and it hadn't been since his days in graduate school that he'd spent so much time on his own. Greg hated being solitary, despised it even, and now the loneliness of the situation was starting to encroach on his mind.

At first he began talking to himself, reminding himself of how great he was and how everybody loved him. He talked about how talented his children were, with one of them now working in Europe. Then he talked about how he has never once visited his son. The poor boy has been all alone in Switzerland for a good three years now, and although he came back to the States for the occasional visit, his foolish father had never deemed it worthwhile to visit him.

After that line of reasoning, there was a small period of silence. A bit of piece for the snow and ice that sat around, that was until he noticed a face-like formation in the ice wall. It was where he had been resting his back just a few minutes prior. Being a gentleman Greg apologized, and went back to silence.

"What's that, who said that?"

"'Tis I Greg, the ice face you so rudely perched your bulbous back upon. It seems you're going a bit mad, and need a friend." The face had a strange voice, one familiar to Greg, but he had a feeling that it wasn't one that he had heard in a long time.

"Do I know you?"

"Know me?! By God's good grace, boy, it's your grandfather!" Ah, of course it was obvious now. He just hadn't recognized him because he was missing his glasses.

"Oh, grandpa Henry! How are you feeling these days, sir? Last I saw you, you were quite deceased. Did you know I'm older now than you ever were?"

"Are you? By God, boy, now that's an accomplishment. It's especially satisfying to see you in such a healthy state. I mean aside from the slight onset of insanity of course, my deepest apologies for that. I feel like I had something to do with it."

"Ah, not a worry in the world, sir; just glad to see you're doing well! Fine real estate you have here, what sort of deity got you into the business of being a face in an ice wall?"

"No deity was involved, just your own fleeting sanity. It is pretty lovely though isn't it?" With that, old grandfather

Henry squeezed himself through the hole in wall and took a tentative seat on the icy floor beside his grandson. "I do miss you, Greg, you and your father. He was a strange child that one. Did I ever tell you story about the big camping trip we took before we moved down to the southwest? Wait, of course I did, or I wouldn't be able to recall it now."

"Ah, yes you did, a true classic! I'm sorry to tell you this, sir, but my dad died last year. It was a heart attack that got him. At the time we weren't on the best of terms, so the last thing I said to him was far more vitriol than love. I blame myself, but honestly it's not like he was sick. How could I know he was going to die before I got a chance to tell him that I love him?"

"Ah, my boy, we're all afflicted with our demons from time to time. I'm sure that son of mine holds no ill will towards ya, especially because he's dead. Now stop trying to have an emotional moment with me, and get out of this damn pit. Back in my day, a man got stuck in a pit he'd be out within five minutes. Don't ya remember your scout training? I don't know how many times I took you boys out to the forest. Every time you just kept screwing around. I'll tell ya what; I'll remind you what to do."

Over the next few minutes Greg worked with the mental fabrication of his grandfather to try and pry himself out of the pit. Despite the fact that his grandfather was completely in his mind, he found that the man gave excellent advice. Alas, after what amounted to a mere five attempts or so, he found himself repeating an act of futility.

"Come on, lad! You can't give up just yet. You're a weakling; it's unlikely you'll survive the night." Apparently at some point in the night, Greg's grandfather had transformed into his Irish gym teacher, Old Sully.

Old Sully was infamous in Greg's high school for being unusually cruel, but at the same time an excellent soccer coach. Apparently a long time back he was a famous player back in Ireland, but moved down to the States for the better weather. He was an odd man, and with Greg being particularly uncoordinated the two never really got along.

"Not now, for God's sakes, if there's one person I never wanted to see again it was you, you old goat. Listen, I'm an adult now, I can make my own choices, and I certainly don't have to listen to you anymore. You ruined my high school years, basically tortured me in your class, and look it didn't get me anywhere! You always said I'd thank you one day, well you're here now, and I'm telling you, there's not a damned thing that I can think of thanking you for. You were a cruel old bastard then, and I was happy to see your obituary in the paper. Hell, I remember all the sentiments that everyone from our class was giving and how the local news even did a little story on your contributions to the community, but you know what, I saw through all that nonsense. You were terrible to me, and sure,

I've come to forgive you, but my God, will I never stop hating your rotten bones."

"Ah, that's exactly what I always wanted you to say, boy! I was trying to pull it out of ya; that fear, a fear of every damn thing that lived. I saw your whiny, pasty, cowardice and I tried to bring out the true strength in ya! Christ on a cracker, lad, did it honestly take ya this long to learn that ya ain't the things that I said ya were?! Have ya finally grown a pair, in what's this, your 58th year? Good on ya, boy, now get your arse out of this pit before I hack it off!"

Greg flew into a rage at the words of his former nemesis. There was no purpose to how he treated him, he was simply a cruel old man that couldn't understand that some people just aren't made for physical activity. Before he knew it, he stood above the old man choking him and slamming him into the wall. He watched as Old Sully's face turned purple as he laughed and laughed at Greg's attempt to harm him.

Old Sully let off one last wink, a signature of his back in the day before he melted into a pile of bones and then dust, right before Greg's eyes.

Afterwards Greg was surprised to find that his mind had miraculously come to a higher state of clarity. He began to look at all his surroundings with a renewed vigor. Everything now had a different purpose, a different reason of being. The cracks in the ice wall that he was once afraid would be his doom, now appeared as elements to climb. There were so many groves and notches that he accidentally carved out while flailing around like a madman in what had been a near perfect, smooth formation beforehand. Even the face in the ice no longer seemed as such, just a mere design that caught his eye. Without hesitation Greg used this clarity to the best of his abilities and divined a way out of the rut he was stuck in, and after ten minutes of climbing and a couple of other trips to grab his belongings, he managed to find his way out.

Nature had been kind to him, there was no snowfall and barely any wind, and if he paid particularly adamant attention he was able to make out the tracks that his guide had left behind in what must have been near a whole day prior. On the walk back to the outpost Greg forgave himself for not clearly seeing what was right in front of him. He also forgave himself for all the pain that he'd let dwell inside his chest since his father's passing, and finally he forgave all of those that had hurt him in the past. It was a true spiritual awakening for a man that didn't believe that such a thing was real or even a possibility.

As he braved that cold with his snow shoes, and his now lackluster collection of salted fish, he looked out into the distance and saw the promising light of the outpost far ahead, there to save him and give him comfort. The walk would be lengthy, but in the end, when it was all over, he'd be a changed man.

Saltman – 1990's meets 1930's for a Couple Minutes

Aside from the children's story this is the shortest tale in the collection. It works as a little love letter to the topic of "forbidden horror", most notably its resurgence in the '90's. The popularization of the genre itself derives from one of my favourite authors in the 20th century, H.P. Lovecraft, and the work that he did to inspire the writers of our more contemporary era, but you'll be hearing much more about him in further tales amongst this collection.

Although '90's "forbidden" style horror has existed since, well, the '90's, I never got into it growing up in that era. Maybe it was my general sheepish nature, or the fact that <u>The X-Files</u> theme song gave me nightmares, but either way it's a mistake that I recently rectified through the magic of modern video streaming services. Having read near the entire collection of Lovecraft's tales, I couldn't help but fall in love with these tales which had lovingly crafted worlds around similar ideals. It's true that well before the '90's, novels and many other media properties used a lot of Lovecraft's ideas and themes, but this wonderful period in the '90's captured it in a way that was so contemporary with the times, the times that I grew up in, that I was inspired to write this little tale.

Saltman

Since this tale, though unfortunately quite short, reminds me of contemporary "mystery horror" so much, and because it does have to do with a bit of my upbringing, I have decided to dedicate this story to my mother. My youth was filled with Stephen King books and similar properties, because of my mom's undying love for them, and it was through these works that I became obsessed with the weird, which in turn is basically the reason behind my creativity. In whole you could really dedicate the vast majority of these works to me Ma, a wonderful person in every way. Though we may have butted heads from time to time, and most likely will continue to on occasion, you are the true origin point to everything good about me, in both an actual biological standpoint as well as a creative one. I love ya, and hope you enjoy this story, though you deserve a whole novel.

Saltman
May, 1938 – Undisclosed Location in Eastern Canada

Reports came in surrounding the appearance of a creature of unknown origin swimming off of the coastline. Some described it as a humanoid while others simply stated it was a giant fish. Although recollections changed from person to person, most claimed that the creature was around 6 or 7 feet in length with thick green scales covered in lichen, or a similar substance. As it swam the creature left behind an oily residue, but the trail dissipated quickly due to the harsh tidal conditions. Chemical analysis of the substance showed that it was a highly saturated lipid with an odd chemical composition. How much the water influenced this sample is unknown, though due to the fact that this was a highly polluted area, the sample should be considered contaminated.

June, 1953 – The Southern Tip of Hudson's Bay (Ontario, Canada)

A humanoid arm washes up on shore. The arm is very similar to that of a large adult man, except the fingers are exceptionally long and webbing interconnects them. Instead of finger nails the hand has long, but thin claws, which proved much denser than the bone in the arm. Similar to the sighting of a creature in the late 1930's, the arm was covered in harsh green scales, which were very hearty, though also extremely light. The bone of the arm was very porous, yet surprisingly resistant to force. Analysis also concluded that the arm had been separated from its host posthumously. If this was the efforts of some prankster, it was extremely well done, for all the tissue was biological. Oddly enough the more logical explanation is that this is the limb of some unknown monstrous species.

News of the arm somehow reaches the press causing a small panic based in curiosity. This leads to a massive increase in the popularity of "Creature from the Black Lagoon" media. Multiple amateur scientists and adventurers investigate the site, disobeying the orders of the Canadian government on both a provincial and federal level. Whatever evidence that may have lain in that lake can now be considered a moot point, as investigators found the area far too disturbed for any reliable conclusions. The rest of the creature's corpse has yet to have been found by any proper authority and probably lies in the hands of some backwoods family in northern Ontario, who lack the appropriate intelligence to return it to the proper authorities.

By the end of its 15 minutes of fame, the arm of the creature was designated to be a part of the "Saltman of

Ontario." Over the next couple of years most people have forgotten about the limb and pass it off as a hoax. Those that refuse to forget the incident are ridiculed by their peers and eventually are sent to mental asylums at the order of the federal government.

February, 1970 – Undisclosed Location in the Far North of Canada

A beast is seen wandering on the ice by locals. They describe the creature as a fish-man, with a somewhat human face, aside from a large gaping maw filled with dagger like teeth. Steam seemed to emanate from the creature, though despite that, the beast left very shallow prints in the snow. The gait of the creature gave off a feeling of desperation as if it were exhausted or starved. Out of fear the locals avoided the beast, and it wandered off into the north.

This event remains hidden by the government, though the tale of a fish beast still circulates heavily among the Native-American population near the sighting.

July, 2011 – St. Catharines, Ontario, Canada

Millionaire author and known eccentric reinvigorates the public on the belief of the "Saltman of Ontario." At this point in time monsters and late 1950's culture are very popular concepts in literature and film, so the public has no problem latching on to the man's ideals. Using his significant influence, the author manages to obtain a small sample of the arm that remains on file. His team, through the use of modern analysis finds that the tissue is not only of an unknown species, but extremely ancient in origin.

He sets a million dollar reward for any additional samples that the public may hold. This leads to mass hysteria, and ends with the murder of four people whose manipulated skeletons were then given to the author in hopes of receiving the reward. The author makes a public apology and continues his efforts in secret from that point forward.

April, 2016 – St. Catharines, Ontario, Canada

Finally satisfied with his results the author comes to the conclusion that the creatures must originate from a deep sea cave. With the aid of marine biologists, botanists in particular, the author surmises a possible location of the whereabouts of the creatures which will go undisclosed in this report.

Journal Entries of the Author in Question

Note that none of the information in the following section of the report is redacted or censored in any fashion, and that only those of the utmost authority should read it, lest they be endangering themselves and allowing the proper authorities to take any action they deem fit against their person, or those they may have contaminated with this information, in order to keep the secrecy of these documents.

We have kept the last three entries only in this document, deeming them to be the only ones worthwhile to the case. All entries went undated, but the current hypothesis based on other physical evidence is that they were written in May of 2016.

Journal of Godfrey Winston

Entry 1

Sasha tells me on a near daily basis now that none of this is worth it. She can't help but rub the memory of those damnable corpses in my face. Whether she reminds me of such things out of mere malice, or if there's an actual point to her torture I'm not sure. When we married she was opposite of cruel, but the stresses of life seem to have sunk their hooks into her pliable flesh. We spend most of our time trying to avoid each other, well I can't speak for her, but it seems a perfectly happy arrangement for both of us.

I remember when the first piece came in, how excited I was to rush it off to the lab, thinking it was the actual missing part from that corpse that washed upon the shore. I remember the biologist as his visage declared his revolt at what he'd found. "What is it?" I said, "Just another hoax?" I was the cause of that poor bastard's death, and the next one, and the one after that, and the fourth. Gods only know how many more bodies there were that never crossed my path. Look at me, turning into Sasha, as her words seem to affect every menial thought that comes to mind.

I know in the end it will all be worth it, but at this time, in this place, I can't help but have my doubts. It seems the defeatism that affects so many of my peers is finally worming its way into my heart. Writing has lost its pleasure, now I do it because it feels like an obligation. I'm having a harder time judging the quality of my own work. The words simply appear, and whether or not they're utter bile regurgitated from the innards of some dying wildebeest I have no clue. I barely edit these things anymore; they pay someone else to do it for me. I don't envy them, whoever they are, and I refuse to meet them and see their disgusted assault of a gaze. Writing brings in the money though, and as this expedition goes on it's only going to get worse for me financially.

On a happier note, the expedition is actually making progress. The marine botanist is a marvel of a human being, she's a true genius. I couldn't even begin to explain how she got the information that she did, but she's localized the possibility of the creature's existence to a mere square kilometer of ocean. Considering how vast the Atlantic Ocean is, the ability to bring it down to a space that concentrated is an amazing feat. She likes to blame her skills on a previous education in forensic studies and geology, a true woman of the Renaissance.

The dive master, this old burly man who seems to be more salt than blood, has had to rework his whole plan. I had originally thought that the find was going to take place closer to the coast and that scuba would likely be a viable option. According to his charts however, we have to deal with a minimum depth of 100 meters, so a submersible is necessary along with a pressure lock. He keeps trying to insist that I let the professional divers deal with the actual excursion, but I always refuse. If anyone is going it will be me. Either way it's starting to really wrack up the bills, he's had to bring in a whole new crew on retainer for when we go on the actual dive. Due to the secrecy of the actual event I've had to pay each person with a substantial down payment before it actually occurs.

In two days the dive will be underway, and I am beyond excited, but preparations call me for now.

Entry 2

The dive seems to have been successful. We got some initial sonar imaging done and there's definitely some kind of complex underwater cave structure below. I don't want to get my hopes too high, but I have a feeling this is it, my ticket to immortality. In a few centuries who's going to remember all my abysmal writings? No, I'll be known as the world's first true monster hunter since old Saint George himself. No time for writing now, the big day sits on the horizon!

<u>Entry 3</u>

I watched as the largest of the group tore her to shreds. No one got out. If this ever reaches the light of day, tell people to keep away. I think they can hear my writing.

End of Journal

July, 2016 – Closing Report

Since the collection of the journal, the Canadian government, in tandem with other organizations which will go unnamed, are now working on spinning the author's disappearance in a different light. Most of the public are of the belief that he is hiding in seclusion from the world given the widely publicized results of his previous call to action that led to the deaths of at least four documented individuals. People who believe otherwise are being treated as pariahs in the media and general social settings.

Attempts to probe the location for information on the "Saltman of Ontario" were brought to the table, but eventually shelved as other projects were considered more deserving of government funding.

Guided – On the Unfortunate Triumphs of Man

I'll be honest; I'm not much of an environmentalist. It's not that I go out of my way to do any harm to the environment, it's just that I'm a generally weak willed human being, and I simply don't have the personal capacity to care as much as I almost certainly should. Unlike me, this story is all about the impact that mankind has had on the environment. Like a lot of my other stories this one takes place in a tundra somewhere in the arctic circle, (I really like the cold for some reason) and surrounds a sort of nature spirit, who I've deemed a guide.

As time goes on the story gets progressively more complex, and really flourishes as both a story of man versus nature and general science fiction. Out of all the stories in this collection I would have to say that this one will probably stand tallest against critics. It may not be my favourite story, but it's probably both the best written and the most poignant and aware of the problems that consist in this contemporary world of ours. For some reason during the writing of this tale, I was much better than I usually am at spot editing, and though it's far from perfect from a grammatical standpoint, I find my editing of it pretty impressive. I generally hate editing and can't wait for the time where I'll be able to hire someone else to do it for me.

Guided

This story is dedicated to all of my friends and family that are much more appreciative than I am of this world that we live on. With just this quality alone, know that you are a much more gallant human being than I. You may think my polite nature and general kindness make me a solid human being, but you're all much more than that.

Guided

It was cold. It was always cold. I sat in that same spot for as long as I could remember, thinking. It was the first time I had seen humans for an untold number of years. I remember how one of them screamed when they saw me sitting there, a woman. At the time I could barely remember what a woman sounded like.

They walked over, talking amongst themselves in a human language, their voices full of fear and confusion. They were lost and I was a guide, so I made a soft noise and turned my head to face them, cracking through the layers of ice that covered my whole body. They jumped at my movement, another scream, this time from many of them.

The leader of the group, a wise man, was soon pulling a blanket out of his backpack and throwing it over my shoulders. A light flashed on the blanket, I had never seen a light other than fire before that point, so I was quite perplexed. Soon the blanket provided a great heat and the ice came to melt off my body. My body was awakening for the first time in a long time.

I threw the device off my shoulders and stretched my back, cracking like a spitting flame. The leader thrust his hand out at me and I accepted it. As I rose the humans began to gather around me. They said their words to me, but I could not answer them. They offered me gifts of food and drink, but I could not consume them.

Guided

One of them wrote of me in a book. This was the first time I had seen a book. They spoke to me some more, making attempts in other languages. Following a number of frustrated attempts to converse with me, one of them pulled out a map. I had never seen a map before, but I knew this land like no other so I quickly learned its purpose. The human pointed to a point on the map with his gloved fingers. It was the village he pointed to, a place far away from my spot, but I knew how to get there.

Soon after, when the humans had composed themselves I began to lead the way after communicating with them as best I could. Night fell quickly, so I built them a fire. As they gathered around the fire they took off their hoods, scarves and goggles, revealing three men and two women. Their scents were panicked and hungry, though their faces revealed them to be well nourished. They could eat from their own stock; I would be doing them no favours that night.

They all slept around the fire, while I stood waiting for the break of day. It was a nice night. I smelled a bear nearby; I remember how I used to care for them. I followed that scent, and it led me to a cave.

The beast was waiting for me, gnawing on the carcass of a seal.

"I'm here."

"Welcome, come in."

I sat beside her; she was strong, well fed. Her summer had gone well. No cubs. Too old, or too young, I wasn't sure. My mind was a lot slower than it used to be, it would be a few days before I was fully awake.

As we sat and talked, the bear told me of her past. She lived a good life, four children, all grown. She wonders how they're doing, what they're doing. I told her I would be sure to tell them of her should we cross paths. She thanked me. Bears speak slowly, with strength, with power. It was a good night to be awake.

As I left to return to the humans I began to wonder how long it had been. When I was last awake there was coast by that cave, covered by hordes of walrus. No place for a bear.

The humans were just as they were when I had left. I reinforced the dying fire, and stood in wait.

As one of them woke they looked up at me, jumping back out of fright. I suppose they thought I would leave. They woke the others.

The smart one began to talk, handing out food and other supplies. He looked to me, spoke slowly. I began to understand some words. Human language is a strange thing, using noises to communicate; loud and unsafe. I learned the words for village, map, fire and gratitude.

They gathered their things.

"Village," I said. They all stopped and stared, strange. I began to walk.

Second day was a nice day, a cold day. Some seemed to question following me; such fools. As they ran back I made sure not to lose them. Lose a human, they die. Eventually we got back on track. The rest of the day was walking, good walking. It would only be a couple days now.

A human started yelling, by then I had forgotten which gender was which, maybe a woman, maybe a man. I heard the word for fire. They were tired, which was laughable. We had rested only half a day prior. Humans hate cold though and it was getting dark, so I built them a fire. There were plenty of trees nearby. Words of gratitude flowed from them, only some directed at me; so much noise, so pointless. They still had plenty of supplies, so I would be doing them no favours that night.

That night I chose to join them, but it quickly made them uneasy. I stayed anyways; fires are nice from time to time, usually a luxury, but a requirement for humans. Perhaps I should have left my gloves on. As my hands hit the light one of them screamed, gestured towards me. Others made exclamations. The smart one grabbed my hand however, a sign of trust in humans. The others calmed.

What was there to fear? My hands, though black as the night, covered in wounds and missing bits of flesh, were completely human looking. It was a strange reaction from strange beasts. The warmth of his human flesh was strange, different than fire. It was a feeling I had not expected to ever feel again.

As they fell asleep I reinforced the fire and went out to the woods. There I would find greater companions than these. I found a rabbit, wrought with fear and hunger. I gathered some food for him, he was on his own. It was his first season out of home. I lay beside him as he ate. We discussed his family. He had two brothers, eight sisters, no lover as of yet. He implored me to send his greetings to any of them if I were to come by them. I promised I would. Before I left to return to the humans I taught him some foraging techniques that he was unfamiliar with, and spent the night stocking his home with food. It was a great night to be awake.

The humans woke up later than they did the day before, perhaps a sign of illness. One of them fell over while we were walking, I decided to carry them. They did not like this. I carried them anyways, though another human tried to assault me while I was doing so. They still feared me.

By the time we stopped for the night I could smell the human village, though it had yet to come into sight. That night was uneventful. The humans went hunting, though they still had plenty of supplies. Fools. They killed a rabbit, probably a relative of the one I had been talking to earlier. It had a similar scent. They threw out the pelt, discarded the organs. It was disgusting,

Guided

terrible, and unforgivable. I cleaned the pelt and sewed it onto my coat. I buried the organs under a growing tree. The last time I awoke humans knew how to respect the forest, now they have grown weak, foolish and distant. I watched as the one with the book wrote more about me. I looked in that book, scratches on paper, words. I had not realized that was what they were at the time. Among the words was a drawing, it was of me. It made me happy. I hadn't seen myself in a long time.

The next day we ran across a bear, the son of the one in the cave. One of the humans shot at him. I grabbed the bullet. It hurt, a lot. The bear ran. Another shot, I caught another bullet. I ran over to the human, took his gun and shot him in the foot. They attacked me, stabbed me, shot me. There was lots of pain. After a while they left me alone, I stood back up, they screamed. The bear was long gone. I picked up the human I injured and began to walk towards the village. More assaults.

Within a couple of minutes we were met by a group from the village. There was so much screaming from them, as they continued to bring me pain. I could smell the animals nearby, they were all afraid. Damned humans were so loud all the time. I dropped the human lightly on the ground; the people from the village helped the others assault me. They knocked me down, tied me up, put me on a sled.

"Gratitude," the smart one said to me.

"Gratitude?!" replied another. Arguing, more noise.

90

The rest of the trip was human talking, a few "villages," a few "gratitudes." The people from the village looked nothing like I remembered. They looked like the humans in the group. Some sort of strange fur, no animal I had ever seen, felt like warm, hard snow.

We were at the village quickly, and they placed me in a strange room. The walls were hard and smooth as ice, but dry. The ground was flat, straight and solid, so strange. I could smell animals, dogs, with a couple cats. They smelt of humans though. No one to speak to, just strange smells. I sat there, tied up, unable to move. I was not ready to rest again. Unlike beasts I never tire so I began to pull on my restraints, they were surprisingly powerful. Before that day I had never found myself unable to escape easily from human devices.

The humans left me alone as they gathered nearby outside the room they had placed me in. I could hear their human speech, though quite muffled, and their smells varied significantly. Some of them reeked of fear, yet in others there was happiness, almost to the point of excitement. It was odd to feel such differing opinions among a single collection of animals; then again humans had always strayed from normalcy.

After a couple hours of pressure the restraints started to get looser, threads getting tired of the strain. The door opened. Food was brought in by the human with the book. It sat across the room from me, making more scratches and occasionally eating from its food. Every couple of minutes it would look up at me before returning to its book. Eventually it walked over to me. It grabbed my scarf and headdress and slowly tugged on them. It used a calming voice in its native language. "You won't want to do that," I said, in the only human language I could remember from an age long past.

It jumped back, opened the door and called out. It looked at me, perplexed. Why? Another human came into the room, older than most. They talked. While they were discussing me the old one said the word "language," in the only human language I knew.

They stared at me. The younger grabbed my scarf again. "I repeat, you won't want to do that," I uttered again. If a human would be afraid of the appearance of my hand than they certainly wouldn't be able to comprehend my face. The older jumped in the air and danced around.

They calmed down. "I speak a little. Do you know this language?" The elder spoke to me. In truth I was a bit confused, but refused to show it.

"You speak too much already."

The elder cheered again; absurd. I hate human tongues. This was the tongue I had learned when the humans first came to settle in my lands. I had not used it on the group earlier as it had never worked on humans in the past aside from my first two encounters with them. Humans soon forgot this language and me with it.

"Do you mind if I talk with you?"

"Yes. I have been assaulted. Humans are fools. I save the lives of your companions, who kill without meaning, only to be captured. I am not an amusement, release me."

"I only understood some. I see you are angry."

"I am not angry, beasts get angry. I am disappointed, but not surprised," the past few times I had been awake I had seen humanity attempt time and time again to dominate this area, corrupting it with a perverted sense of superiority manifested through attempts of dominance.

The older human jumped around with joy. More absurdity, more noise. It raised a black box to its mouth, spoke. Only creatures as strange as humans would speak to boxes.

"Bring in a smart beast," I told it.

"Apology?" It was making no sense. This human treated the language I knew like its own.

"Bring a human then. Bring in 'gratitude' human."

The older one was confused, the one with the book talked to him. As they were talking humans came in, one carrying a black box. The smart human was not with them. The two other humans ended their conversation; the one with the book left under the elder's instructions.

Guided

I could feel my bindings giving way. It would be a matter of minutes. A big human grabbed me, pulling me to my feet by the pit of my arm. I stood. Fools, these humans think I'm a threat. The older one follows close behind as the group of humans leads me out into some other building. More smooth walls and floors. Some walls are see-through, like ice, but perfectly clear. I break free of my ropes, drop to all fours and begin to run from the group. The older one shouts. Men try to chase me down. I had had enough of these humans. As far as I was concerned my job as their guardian was done, they were clearly in strong enough standing to fend for themselves.

Before long they are far behind me, and I head deep into the forest. I smell bear, not the one from earlier.

I find him at a creek, fishing. "Greetings," I say to him.

"Welcome, come in. Careful, there are humans nearby."

"Yes, I just came from them; the worst of beasts."

The bear stopped for a second. "They won't follow you here?"

I laughed, "Humans can't smell, they are weak."

"Humans don't need to smell anymore, old one. Look." He leaned his head toward me to reveal a small box attached to his ear. A blinking light came off it. "They follow me with this. Why? I don't know."

"You know much and more about humans, wise beast. Tell me of them, I have slept for many years. It seems every time I awaken they get stranger."

As we sat the beast told me of the exploits of humanity; how they were not of a single mind, working as both predators and saviours to the creatures of the wild. The bear told me of his capture, which he had first attributed to his assured demise, but ended up being an event that helped his own survival. In the days prior to his capture he was viciously bitten by a small pack of seals who worked to defend one of their brethren from the bear's jaws. In the following days he could barely move, managing to reach his cave through adrenaline alone. By the time that the humans found him he had gone nearly a week without more than a few laps of cave water.

Unable to properly fight back, the bear submitted to the human's capture knowing his death was assured none the less. To his surprise the humans didn't taste of his flesh, but mended him through means he had yet to comprehend. Since those days amongst the humans they had come to check on him every couple of months or so.

This bear was a true creature of the wild though and ensured me that if the time comes he would gladly feast on them. There are no favours in the world of hunters, merely gifts that seek no reciprocity. While I may be able to accept such returns from a more peaceful creature, among bears and wolves all was fair, and I wouldn't have expected any less.

I would stay with the bear for a few nights after that. As he knew my true nature, he respected me enough not to make an attempt on my own mortality. He was a wise creature, and I hold him in fondness, though I would certainly never see him again. Each night he would tell me more stories on the nature of man, warning me that any of their kindness would be replaced with violence in time. The greatest impact that his stories had on me was the realization that man had grown to be far more complex than I remembered; though they roamed the lands as predators there was an odd kindness to them, born of curiosity rather than an inherent peace. The exploitation that I had witnessed in my encounters with them in the past had become balanced with a sort of conservancy that reminded me of my own species in times long past.

Taking the advice of the bear to heart I decided to make my return to the human lands, submit and observe their ways. The bear told me that nature was at a balance, that it was humanity that truly needed my assistance. Their furs were born of manipulation, not of animals, but the earth itself, and though they were at the height of resourcefulness they lacked the proper instinct. He had seen humans die from exposure, watched as they wandered into claimed territories without a proper means to defend themselves. He also asked me to help them in retribution for the assistance they provided him, for though predators hold no favours they can still respect the notion of aid.

As I reached the human camp the area reeked of a tainted blood, a kind of smell that only emanates from the diseased. When I drew near to the site I followed the smell to the back of the village. Though I had originally planned to hide from human eyes until I could obtain a safer position from their persecution, it was clear stealth wouldn't be necessary. By the time I had reached the source of the scent I had yet to view a single human.

Before I had reached the end of the village I had expected death, but what I found still managed to surprise me. It was not tainted blood that created the smell, but the combination of normal blood and tainted flesh.

"Brother?" I called to the creature that sat gnawing on the bones of its victim. It turned its head to face me, opened its mouth and howled in the air. It was a guide, much like me, but it had lost its furs, and abhorred rivets of bone or some sort of strange rock protruded from its naked body. "What are you doing awake? This is my time, sister."

It stank of disease, toxicity and waste. As I approached, it leapt away bounding into the wilderness. Before this moment I had never seen a feral guide, if that's what it was. Though its body reminded me of my species, that horrid stench nullified my ability to identify it. This was turning into quite the strange awakening.

The human corpse was torn and flayed. The skin splayed out much akin to the work of a hunter interrupted. Perhaps the humans at this village were more malevolent than I thought. There were two trails of blood, one in which the human was dragged to the spot and another that was left by the blood covered guide when it fled. Since I saw little point in following my brethren, though I admit I was very curious about them, I decided to investigate the other trail. The blood here was that of something dragged, streaks lining the snow. There were no other prints.

The streaking trail ended in a human building, culminating in a large red puddle at its end. The area smelled of humans, alive and in fear. It was all rather strange. There was very little blood outside of the trail and the small pool gathered at the end, even the wall adjoined to the puddle was clean. Looking back at the whole endeavour, I should have probably looked into the matter further, but my goal during my time awake was to protect those humans that looked to me for assistance.

I found them in a faraway corner, armed with weaponry that they liberally applied to me. It was very painful. Among the group there were five that I recognized, but well over double that in total. Among them was the elder human that spoke the language I had learned in a time long past. "Beast, hear my words," I called to him. "Tell me what has happened in this place since I last fled."

The elder stepped forward, though the others tried to convince him otherwise. With him another human stood, well-armed. "You are the one that left? That ran?"

"Yes. I learned of your benevolent ways from a creature in the wilderness; a great white bear. I have come back to provide you with the aid you need. Now tell me, what has happened here?"

"I don't understand all of what you said, my apologies. I did hear that you want to help." He turned to face his human compatriots, spoke to them in their human language. Some seem relieved by his words, while others held protest. After a few minutes of discussion, the elder turned back to me. "A creature unlike anything we humans know attacked us. Many are dead throughout the village."

"Yes, I saw the creature, and even I am unsure of its origins. It is ancient, much like me, but full of rage. It is wrought with disease and foul taint, so much so that I was unable to talk to it. Its mind is outside the realm of nature. Now follow me."

As I herded the humans to safety a scent struck me. There was another human, still living, along with many of the dogs that lived amongst them. I must have been too transfixed on the tainted scent before to smell it. I knew this human; it was the smart one from the group I had brought over.

I followed the scent, the humans following close behind. Eventually the smell just stopped. I stood still, pondering its location. Soon after I stopped moving one of the humans following me came around in front of me and placed their hand on my chest. A couple others followed their actions. All three of them stood in front of me. I soon came to realize this was an act meant to inhibit me, one based in hostility. I ignored them, humans are odd creatures, offended by the strangest of actions, and at the time I had no plan to follow through and heed their request, there was a human to aid. I stood there, looking around for a clue of the human's whereabouts. The creatures were below me. Of course, it made perfect sense, that's why the trail stopped. You must forgive my slow conclusion, at the time I had no idea that humans were capable of building structures beneath the ground, and since we were not on top of an ice sheet I had no reason to think that anything could be below us.

At this realization I fell to the ground, clearing the snow to get access to the ground. One of the humans tried to restrain me, but to no avail. Others joined in the attempt, but were just as unsuccessful. Much like their act of prohibition earlier I saw no need to burden myself with understanding their mannerisms and kept on. What I found was a true oddity however. There was no ground beneath the snow but what seemed to be some sort of hollowed sheet of rock. I stomped on the rock causing a sound similar to the striking of a rotted out log, but deep and enclosed. The humans yelled toward the ground while a few others tried to restrain me, trying to pull me towards them. When the humans tried to restrain me before I allowed them, knowing it was, in their minds, a matter of securing their own safety. This time however, they were disallowing me from saving one of those that I was bound to protect, something that I would not allow.

Before long a creaking erupted from the ground, and a large gap opened right in front of me. Horror struck the faces of the humans, an abject fear, that confused me. Unable to restrain me I stepped through the gap, following the staircase down. The humans ran in front of me, yelling towards the interior of this underground while others tried to hold me back. I pushed through my would-be inhibitors, causing as little damage to them as possible. Some of them even latched onto me, their feet dragging along the floor in an attempt to slow me down, which did manage to have some impact on my movement. By the time I reached the bottom of the staircase another smell hit me, very faint yet familiar, it was the scent I knew best, my own, but it wasn't coming from me. Curious I unlatched the humans that had clung themselves to me, unfortunately breaking a few of their arms in the process. They would be fine though, no permanent damage was done, and certainly nothing I couldn't mend for them.

I saw the dogs first, eight in total sleeping throughout the room, most pressing their backs against the walls. Then I saw the smart human, hidden against the back wall, a collection of humans from those that followed me here were guarding him. The elder human, the translator, ran up to the group. He was situated behind me, but he wasn't one of the people that held me back. The smart human and the elder spoke, and eventually the smart one left the protection of the group. The smart one began to speak to me in his tongue, his tone was frantic. He ran up to me and fell to his knees, begging something from me. Prostrating himself, much like a wolf who knows he's been defeated. Needless to say I was confused. I looked to the elder human.

"What is this he's saying to me? Why show all this fear towards me?"

The elder spoke with his head bowed, "Look," and hit something, a small circle on the back wall. I felt the smart human cling to me, weeping human tears.

The wall shifted, splitting down the middle like cracking ice, and pulling itself apart. The humans began to flee to the outside. It was the scent from earlier, my scent; it erupted from the splitting wall. I laid a hand on the human attached to me who promptly released himself. As the wall separated more and more the realization finally came to me. They had guides, not one or two, but all of them. They were still sleeping. Their furs had been torn from them, some of them were even split open, their innards exposed to the open air. Recalling my memories I began to count them. There were 34, two missing from the total, including me. It was so strange to see them like this. It had been millennia upon millennia since I had seen another of my kind, yet here they all were, as motionless as trees. Looking down at my own hands I had come to the realization that I forgot what I looked like underneath these furs, yet we all looked the same. There I was; the front of me, the back of me, even inside of me. I turned to the elder.

"Now I understand," the elder looked at me with sad eyes. "You woke it up, that creature, the one that killed all those humans." I nodded to the collection of my species. "Humans are curious, you always have been. It's a true shame what you've done here, but I understand."

"What can we do to get you to forgive us?" the elder was desperate for answers, he feared me, feared for the future of his people.

"Do not worry about my forgiveness you are in no danger from me. Do you think I offend this easily? Did you fear my vengeance at the destruction of my species?" Watch this." I wandered over to one of my brethren that had the interior of their bodies exposed. The skin was held in place by some sort of

103

structure. As I tore the containing structure apart sparks flew, it confused me to say the least. After the structure was torn from its flesh, my brother quickly sewed back together. "See? No harm done to my people. Even the one you awoke is in no danger. So, no forgiveness is needed. In fact I must say that it's pretty nice to see them all again, it had been a long time." I looked down towards the smart human. "Gratitude," I spoke to him in his own language.

The smart human was confused, but wrapped its arms around me before adorning itself with some of those strange furs and retreating to the outside. The elder I asked to stay.

"In two moons time I will fall asleep once more. Do you know the word for years?"

"Yes, I know years. I know all the numbers too."

"Alright, in six years' time another one of my people will awaken. It is unlikely to be the one that you forced awake, so know that until that time it is unlikely that that one will stop its violence. It is possible that I am able to stop it and return it to sleep.

"After I return to sleep do not awaken another, not even me. If I fail to return it to its slumber before my time is up then you will need to wait six years for another one of us to awaken, and that's only if it thinks you need its guidance. I will try my best elder human, but I cannot guarantee your safety."

"Will you stop it for us? That is if we promise not to awaken another."

"You don't need to promise anything to me. I am here to aid you; I am merely giving my advice. I need you to hide these humans. Know that if I succeed in stopping my brethren you may gladly seek my knowledge." The elder and I left together; the humans were no longer a priority, so I left them to their own protection.

My sibling was full of blight and disease. The toxins did not have enough time to properly expel from their body before they were awoken. Based on the degree of toxicity emanating from them, their awakening was a long time in the future, at least a century. Their scent was absent from my senses, so I was forced to return to the site of the dead human and follow their trail from there.

The human body was gone, flowers lay in the spot where it had been not too far ago. I was unsure where the corpse had gone. Its blood long frozen would leave no new trail. I hoped that the humans had taken the body, knowing the importance of their death customs, but it wasn't a certainty.

I followed the bloody trail that my brethren had left. In the woods the trail disappeared from the ground, prints and drips pressed against the trees instead. Following their trail led me to a stream where the scent had finally caught to me. This could only mean that they smelt me just as clearly, though whether their feral mind could discern it was a different concern all together. The scent led me far, ending at a body of water, a small but deep bay often frequented by seals, their prey and their predators. I dove in, my muscles morphing and expanding under the water's surface. Within minutes my body adapted itself and I sped through the water. I could sense the movements of it, and breathed in the blood that circulated in the water.

There it was flopping around through the water, its body not properly adapted. This was the perfect circumstance for me. Its intoxicated mind unable to properly orient itself to the environment left it vulnerable. It could be hours until it was in a proper state, while it only had minutes before I would put it back to sleep.

I had been in my sibling's situation once, a long time ago. At a point in time where humanity had yet to be, and we guides were beings of greater influence in this world. I had fallen asleep on a volcano, which became active while I rested. I remember awaking in a pool of magma, my thoughts a garbled mess of rage and confusion, the unending pains inside my mind. I pulled myself out of the depths of the earth, half my body pumped full of rock, while the other tried to reform around it. I destroyed everything, massacring families, demolishing forests, until one of them found me restrained me and put me to sleep. I would go on to miss my next cycle, still in recovery from the incident, but when I finally awoke I was in a state of bliss, with double the recovery time I didn't have an ounce of disease in me. It was truly glorious.

I eventually latched on to them, using the protrusions sticking from its back. It was the same materials that the structure was made from. As they flailed wildly I watched as its body kept trying to repair itself, just like mine, it was unable to destroy the material. I broke the protrusions off, but yet the body struggled. I tore it open, and ended up pulling out part after part of horrific formations the humans had installed. Many of the parts were clawing on to its organs, making their way all throughout its body. By the end of the ordeal my sibling was little more than a husk, slowly repairing, the progress inhibited by the disease in its mind. I finished it much as my sibling finished me, by tearing off the head, which immediately fell back to sleep.

Its body sunk down, disintegrating into what would amount to fish food. By the time I reached the shore its shoulders had already started to form. A remarkable feat considering how slow its reconstruction had been as it was still awake. I hid the remains in a nearby tree, making sure there was ample room for reconstruction. As I sat there beside my sibling's sleeping mind, I felt something that I'm not sure I had ever felt before. It was similar to how one feels when they're concerned, but it was concern over me.

Those humans had managed to awaken my sibling, something once achieved only by the greatest of natural forces. My mother had told all of us that the only way we could wake were if it was deemed so by a force far stronger than ourselves. What use is there in protecting and guiding a species capable of feats so strong that they dwarf our own? I was so stricken by this new feeling that I simply couldn't bring myself to return to the humans. I felt a doom that I had never felt before.

It was among the forest that I would spend the remainder of my waking days, discussing nature, family and survival with the truly civilized beings of this world. I returned to some old friends I had met along the way. I managed to find the bear mother's children, three were happy and healthy, and one was even in the midst of fostering a family of her own. The other I couldn't find though one of the siblings told me they had died many moons ago. I managed to help creatures in need along their way, feeding and sheltering them. Even those that were well off tended to be grateful for my company, it was a pleasant time. It was the last time I would see the light of day, feel the winds or even smell another creature.

Now I am awake again, but all I have are my thoughts, as my will and freedom is owned by the humans that I had saved so many times in the past. I await the day my mother returns.

Orthopraxy: In the Beginning – A Start of a Series

In general I'm a fellow with a lot of interests, most of which are relatable to pretty much anyone else. One of the things that have always tickled my fancy that other people find a little strange however is my obsession with ancient religious beliefs. There was a point in my life where I was so interested in the topic that it was what I specialized my education in it, "Pre-Christian Religious Tradition", a title I made up. This story, which I like to call "In the Beginning", is the start of a series of short stories about the lifestyles that surrounded ancient religions and their cultures, as well as those that opposed them. I decided to name the series "Orthopraxy", meaning the correct actions in the eyes of God, or in this case a deity in general. The potential for this series excites me, because there are just so many topics that can be covered, and I'm looking forward to what it will become in the future.

To start the series, I thought I might as well take it off from a logical point, that is, the beginning. "In the Beginning" takes place in an ancient eon where man was far from the top of the food chain, and where beasts were the ones that ruled the Earth. Religion as a concept was relatively new, as humanity had just started to evolve into the capacity to form cognitive ceremonial functions outside of a utilitarian lifestyle.

The inspiration for this story is a particularly special one for me; the relationship between me and my late canine companion Kera. Never have I met a greater being, and I doubt I ever will. Out of any animal I've ever met, human or otherwise, I have yet to meet someone with as much personality, and just pure unadulterated sass. More human than a human, and almost more cat than dog, but with all the love and majesty of her fellow species brethren, our friendship is something that will never leave me.

Out of all the stories in this collection this is the one that is most similar to the writing style that I implemented in "The Sagas of Windholm", my previous book. Much like in that work, the writing here is direct, "telling rather than showing" as is the common writing trope. For a lot of people this style tends to rub them the wrong way, thinking that it has no place in modern written styles, but perhaps that's the point for these types of tales. I'm attempting to bring them out of modernity as much as I can. I've always had this primal interest in the lands before modernity. There was no teacher, or specific moment, or any sort of singular event that led to my love of this topic, but alas I adore it.

This one was a lot of fun for me to write, even with all the hassle of editing it all. I do really hope you enjoy it as much as I do, even if the topic is based quite a bit on my personal interests.

Orthopraxy: In the Beginning

They had always said two things to me, those in my tribe. That I was born blessed, and that the future of all of life would rest on my shoulders. That was many winters ago though, and now I have often found myself doubting the words of my elders. Life had been harsh to She and I, but unlike many, we were still living, breathing and fighting to make every effort count.

That cold, brutal land was kind to no one, this I knew, but I, even amongst the greater suffering of others, had never felt myself to be a creature of higher circumstance. I may have been strong, stronger than any of my kind, but in that same instance I knew my mind was weak. There had been some in my tribe, in that time long past, who could speak and communicate amply with all manner of beast. Aside from She there was no one outside my tribe that I could understand, and often even comprehend.

That day we found ourselves walking through a valley of which two mountains climbed deep into the abyssal sky on either side. We had expected this place to be shielded from the cold and in one way we were correct in this assumption. There was no wind, but we found that this place like all the others I had seen was not exempt from the bitter frost of winter, and the pain that came from such a factor. We trudged on through the snow; the howl of beasts from far away no longer had any meaning to either of us. If they were to come upon us, then they were. A tribe lived nearby these mountains. Over the crest of the mountain set to our left we would occasionally see smoke from a pyre, and some of the howling would be produced by the creature that is born and bred in weak, hairless bodies, the one that I was embarrassingly a part of. At the same time this was a sign of hope. These beasts were capable of trade and diplomacy on a scale that no other could achieve. They're also some of the easiest for She and I to dominate and slaughter, thinking their stones and spears hold true weight outside of hunting plant eaters.

As we got closer and closer to reaching the end of the valley, which rested in front of us a few hundred meters away, I looked to She and motioned towards the smoke in the distance. She bared her teeth, but emitted no sound. This was an obvious sign that she believed violence was the best course of action. In many ways I agreed with her, but yet the temptation for a few moments of peace with others of my kind was too tempting for me not to rebuke her. At the best of times She was the opposite of agreeable, so I could never count on her efforts being in the same vein as mine, but at the same time I saw a certain peace in her expression that seemed to convey agreement, no matter how reticent.

Curious enough upon coming close to the edge of the valley there was a spot with a few winter berries sprouting from the ground. I couldn't wholly recall if this variety was safe to eat, for winter berries tended to be quite the rarity among these parts. It wasn't until She started to eat them that I decided to indulge myself. Food was rare, especially plants, so it had been several days since either of us had eaten anything. The fact that She ate the berries at all was sign enough that she was hungry, it was rare for her to eat anything other than meat when the opportunity arose.

Our initial thought was to head towards the tribe that lay to the left of the mountain range, for that was the place most likely to be our source of food and shelter for at least a night's span. At the same time darkness had already struck, and it was about the time that a fire was necessary. Looking around by moonlight alone we quickly found an alcove that would at least partially cover us from the wind and keep a bit of shelter over our heads. Though we had a fire just the day beforehand it felt a near eternity since I had encountered heat's embrace. I had been alive on this earth for almost twenty winters, the majority of which I had been lighting my own fires and cooking my own food. Sometimes it brought me shame to realize that I was once a helpless burden amongst my people for my first couple years of life.

Quickly I formed a fire with the wood that I had been carrying on my back. Luckily I had gathered plenty since we had last left a forested area, and I managed to grab some foliage

Orthopraxy: In the Beginning

from the bushes and shrubs that lay in the valley. She wasn't always one for fires, but even she had to submit out of the bitter cold for tonight. Now that we were out of the valley the biting wind was back, ready to assault either of us as soon as we set foot outside the alcove that the deity had provided for us. It was then that I realized I should be thankful for such a spot, and brought the creator off of its place on my pack. Through it all, the all-powerful had stayed in perfect condition. True, every few days I did need to retrace some of its markings, and there had been that one day where a tooth had been chipped which left me immobile for nearly a week's time, but it's perfection couldn't be doubted. In comparison I looked at my own body, the two fingers I had lost to the cold, and most of my toes wouldn't move anymore after a decade of injuries. Along my arms and chest I was riddled with scars provided to me by those of my species, with my legs and hands strewn with the bites and claw marks of those other beasts. I was imperfect, but it would be through my imperfection that I would protect the deity. The being of all importance was the only truth one could rely on out here.

After I praised the mighty one, the wind started to decrease, as could only be expected for an ardent follower and protector such as myself. She and I used this opportunity to take to hunting, though by that point the sun had begun to rise, so it wouldn't be possible to find a creature in the throes of sleep. It was the first time in near on a week that we had entered an environment where other life could easily be found. Within an hour we had found a small creature that put up a significant fight. She and I split the spoils of our hunt and decided that a little over half would do enough to fill our bellies for the day. It was a strange circumstance that we were wounded by such a small being, it's often surprising to find our own blood amidst the carnage that lies in the snow. The creature had claws befitting a true warrior beast, sharper than any knife my own species could make.

After we ate I looked more closely at our wounds, applying some herbal remedies that my father had instilled in my memories in a time so long past. She was always reluctant to let me near her wounds, but over time we had begun to trust each other. In those early days I would often need to force the remedy on her, and she wouldn't communicate with me for hours. I don't know how long the two of us had been together, but it must be at least two winters worth of time, that being our third. To be true, it was rare for that part of the world to be out of winter, so the years tended to get lost on me. I remember my father telling me that he had once travelled to a land where the grass showed for the majority of the year, where snow was a rarity.

It shames me that I couldn't remember any of the words to my birth language. I regret the fact that in those early years on my own I was too weak of mind to practice my words. Who knows how many of my kind I could've communicated with over the years, how many fights and wounds I could have avoided. It's true that most tribes spoke entirely different languages from their neighbours, though the closer they were the more alike the languages would be. There was no time to think of such things though, not then, as I sat with She by the fire that I had just rebuilt.

In the distance we could smell the cooking of flesh, a feat of my own kind's engineering. The stench could only be coming from the source of that pyre smoke that we had seen prior. I made the decision that we would move over to the tribe after our rest.

With our wounds healed we began to make the trek over to their side of the mountain. We imagined that it wouldn't be too far of a walk, especially if we decided to climb the mountain to take a shortcut. Luckily the ascent was far from steep, but it was still a long walk over. At the highest point that we would come to there was a tight outcropping of trees in which we could take shelter. The convenience was unheard of, an ease of life which could have only been provided by the creator itself. It was due to this stroke of luck that we managed to stay relatively comfortable throughout this journey, so I made sure to spend the night set deep in prayer to the great one that I had devoted my life to. I looked at its teeth, which were the sharpest I had ever seen, and the rock which encased it and kept it preserved for generations to come. As I held it in my hands I could only help but feel amazed at my luck and the importance of my duty. As I grew up my father told me that I would be the most important creature on the whole of the earth, he always told me I was born for it.

I remember how when I was still a child I towered over everyone else in the tribe, including my own parents. As I looked at them sometimes I could sense their fear, but more often it was admiration that I saw in their eyes. We were a great tribe, one of the largest in the land, so much so that we had multiple outcrops, making our language and lifestyle the most populous in the region. My father was the head of it all for a long time, a man, made old and wise by time, the oldest human that I had ever seen, being over 70 at the time of his death. I was his 12th child, though less than five had made it over the age of 8. Since he was 15 years old he had been the head shaman of the tribe, making him the most responsible person for the well-being of the people under him. He wore elaborate dress, made from the skins and feathers of as many beasts as he could muster. His face mane stretched near to his knees by the time that he was dead, something that was often considered quite dangerous because of how such a thing could get in the way during a fight or a hunt. A man with as much power as him certainly had his enemies; people looking to enter a place of power would have to come to him for permission, something that most people resented to say the least. With all his enemies it wasn't internal strife that led to his death though.

As the night fell, She and I ate what remained of the creature we had defeated the day before, and felt surprised at how much progress we had made over a single day. My prayers were deep, though they revealed nothing of the future, but signified that the actions I was taking were right by the creator of all. Aside from that it was a dull night. She woke up several times in the night and traversed the area around the tree line, but always came back, something that once surprised me quite significantly. It was quite outstanding how far our relationship had come since we first met; both outcasts of our tribes, made strong by nature and our uncommunicative natures. Before we had met up the loneliness was palpable, each day dragged on in silence of both mouth and mind, and though She couldn't make many noises that weren't based in rage, the connection between us on a personal level made me become quite addicted to her presence.

I remembered in that night the first days that the two of us had spent together. Each night we both stayed wide awake, expecting the other to attack as soon as our guard was down. During the days when we travelled we stayed a fair distance away from each other, always looking over our shoulders and keeping focus on one another's presence. Of course we fought, quite often in fact. Many of our own scars had come from those early fights. It was the fights that truly sealed the bond though. Both of us were creatures with great strength that would resort to fighting before doing anything else. We both knew our place in this world, as killers, hunters and problem solvers. Together we couldn't help but imagine that we'd be near invincible, especially after seeing how one another fought.

I may not have been the smartest of my species, but I had a masterful talent to adapt to the situation, the efficiency of weapons and tools were obvious to me. I was quick to make spears, fashioning them from bones and wood every night, lighter ones to throw, bigger ones to stab. I carried the throwing spears in a small leather quiver that I kept on my side. Unfortunately I can't say that I made such a great piece myself, it was given to me by a dying man after I had given him some food to ease his passage. He was a friend that travelled with She and I for quite a while, the only friend of my species that I've made for any notable length of time since the destruction of my tribe. On my other side is where I carried my club and my axe, both made from massive stones that no ordinary beast could carry in one paw. I only liked to use these when the situation got up close and personal, for though they tended to do less damage than the spears, they were the only means of killing another creature in a single blow if they were currently on the attack. The axe was also a handy tool that made for the building of fires, so I tried to use that less than the club as to have less need to sharpen it.

Another lesson that I was taught when I was a child that came not from my father, but instead the lead hunter of the tribe, was that sharpening a weapon also meant reducing its mass and its density, which were both dangerous to the longevity of the device. Unlike spears which could be made a dime a dozen, finding a rock suitable for a person my size that also held the right shape, was a rare find to say the least. The rocks also had to be loose, for even my strength can't best the elements of nature when the creator wants me defeated. Not all things in the natural world were meant to be used by humans, not even by one as important as me. This was a fact of life that the creator had made obvious on our journey together.

On my back lay the most important elements to my survival, including food, repair materials, my large spears and of course the deity itself, which always saved us from certain death. Currently I didn't have nearly as much weight on my back as I would have wanted. We were lacking food entirely, though luckily we had eaten, and I'd used the last of my leather a couple of weeks past to repair my outfit. The only thing we weren't lacking in was bone. The spears that I was currently using proved to be quite hardy to say the least, I couldn't tell if this was a sign that I was getting better at building them, or if this was a sign of the deity's commitment to our cause of survival.

The sun had not yet rose when I woke from my slumber, another hindrance of winter, but the two of us needed to get moving before hunger began to set in to a significant degree. I woke up She and got bit on the hand for it. Annoyed not by the pain, but by the fact that I'll have to clean the wound, I picked She up and threw her. It never hurt her, but it always shocked her, having never met another human that could even attempt to commit such an act. She realized her mistake and we quickly moved on. The day, or pre-day, as it could be called, was warm to a surprising degree. Not to the level of summer in the south that my father had told me about, but one of the warmer days that She and I had seen in a long time. As we travelled the day got warmer, at its height, I could barely see my breath, and not out of lack of trying.

Feeling the snow weak beneath my feet, I knew this would be a difficult trek. Once the snow got high enough I could sink in significantly, luckily the slope of the mountainside was enough to deter any significant depth. The most pervasive problem with the deep levels of snow wasn't so much the hindrance, as it was the friction and therefore damage that would be inflicted on my clothing. If the snow reached above

Orthopraxy: In the Beginning

my waist, a secondary problem became relevant in that the possibility of losing items became much more likely, though with my height, that depth was a notable rarity. I found myself wondering once or twice over those years whether or not my stride, speed and strength could be altered to reduce damage, and tried various techniques, none of which seemed to make any true difference, at least any that I could note.

When you live where I lived, by yourself, for as long as I have, you learn the importance of adaptation. You have to learn how to experiment and work to create the best possible advantages. In truth, I often find myself talking about all the things that my father has taught me, but I have learned as much and more on my own. He may have taught me the importance of the hunt, but he never taught me the skills that I needed to master it. It was through my own experiences that I learned the importance of being distrusting of mankind, who will often choose manipulation over violence, which I've always found both more noble and less dangerous for other species, and those like myself who favour action. Enough disparity though, it's time that I returned to the action at hand.

As we travelled the snow got deeper, far more than I was expecting, and I thought that I could feel a couple perforations starting to form in the leathers and furs that covered my legs. Luckily they were all quite a few layers deep, so I at least wouldn't be at an immediate risk of frostbite on that day. She always found the snow much easier to navigate, even though she was far from my own height. I watched as she bounded through all of it with such ease that you would have sworn that there was none there. I knew that in many ways she was my physical superior, agility being the most notable difference in traits. None the less I trudged on, watching as She occasionally looked back at me, as if perplexed by my lack of speed, though I had a feeling that she was doing so to insult me, a common practice for her.

As we began to descend down the hill we eventually came to see the human village that we had been heading towards this whole time. They were set in a valley at the mountain's base, and I could even see from that distance that there was a source of running water. It seemed that they were more well off than I imagined they would be. I made sure that She didn't begin an assault before I properly understood the lay of the land in front of us. There was something about this place that reminded me of something that I couldn't quite recall. From where I was standing there wasn't much to see. Their shelters were sturdy enough, built quickly for movement, but the only notable element was a large pyre in the center of the settlement. At the time I had no idea what it was, or what it could possibly be used for, the only thing that crossed my mind was how much of a waste of wood such a structure was. There was no way that such a massive installation could be used to cook food, well literally of course it could, but it would be extremely inefficient and there was no way that a settlement this size would have lasted this long making acts like this. I began to get more and more curious the longer I looked at it. I couldn't figure out what it could have possibly been used for.

I motioned to She that we should approach quietly and safely, only attack them if we have to. I put my spear away and hollered at them to make sure they knew of my approach. I used the symbol that the people of my tribe used to display peace, but I doubted that they would react to it though, as I was quite a distance away from anyplace that would recognize the designs and expressions that I had been born into.

Unlike the words of my people, the symbols had stuck with me. I'd had to use them quite often during those first few years after I separated from my family. They were well used by the people and tribes that wandered the landscape by my birthplace, even though most of us were divided by separate languages. To my surprise only one person looked up at me, and they all but ignored me for a few minutes until they went underneath a shelter and came back with two men, burly fiends with spears. The other villager pointed up to our position and one of the men yelled up at me. I couldn't understand them, but it sounded peaceful enough, a sort of warbling sound. We continued to make our descent, She a fair distance behind so as

126

to maintain peace. Due to her violent nature she couldn't be trusted around those that have only been endangered by her kind in the past.

When we were a mere couple of minutes away the whole of the tribe seemed to ready for our arrival. By my count there were no more than ten people amongst them as well as a few other beasts that kept them company. Seeing that there were other beasts around provided me a significant deal of peace. To me, as well as She, the sight of my kind living cooperatively with other creatures was a sign of intelligence and a desire for diplomacy. It meant that they understood that other creatures were worthwhile, a very common state for a large number of creatures, but these beings occasionally viewed themselves as superior due to their adaptability and higher degree of intellect, a dangerous mindset to have. This was the first good sign, the second being that only two members were holding spears, and even then it was just at their sides. There had been many occasions in the past where not only would spears be brandished, but javelins would have already been tossed at me by this point. Javelins were effective against a target as big as me so having them tossed at me brought out a great degree of rage. They were one of the few things I was afraid of when it came to dealing with my kind, which compared to most of the beasts I come across were generally weak and fragile.

Orthopraxy: In the Beginning

Fear on a whole was one of the most important aspects of existence in that time period. To be afraid was not a weakness, but a form of intelligence. For most beasts, a fear of death was all that kept them alive, and a fear of pain would often keep the world from falling apart. Though when it comes to me, my fear of death was only there because I knew the creator would not survive without me. I feared pain because it brought me into a rage that I often couldn't comprehend, very less control. It was always an unknown factor as to how much danger I could cause when enraged, if I were to ever cause damage to the creator or injure She then my life would be worth less than I could comprehend. I used to think that She was an unimportant factor in my life, but I realized that I had come to a point where I couldn't imagine a life without her assistance and companionship.

Those were the thoughts that came to mind at that time, so I was beginning to feel a strange anxiety, one that I wasn't used to, to say the least. I looked back at She, worried for her life for no apparent reason. She wasn't in danger in any way, and even if the people of the tribe had seen her they had yet to make any moves against her safety, but the fear was there all the same. I began to act with greater caution, though not enough to show that I had any fears. I signaled to She that she should hide, or at least move with caution. This was a signal that the two of us hadn't used in a long time, so my hope was that she remembered it, though I couldn't help but doubt it.

When I reached the village I dropped all my weaponry on the ground, and prepared my belongings for trade. The villagers were talking amongst themselves, some whispering some shouting at one another and myself. An old man walked up to me and touched me on the arm. I hadn't seen this man from afar, but I was amazed at his age, I had to assume that he was at least in his 60s. I returned the favour and touched his arm back, which I could only hope was a sign of peace, if not respect. To the best of my ability I motioned to the elderly man that no one was to touch the creator, and through his wisdom he seemed to have figured out my meaning and made a motion of agreement. Our conversation went well, with me only having to use a few threats. With each motion I made the elderly man turned to what seemed to be the head warrior of the village and spoke to him in their guttural language.

Looking at the warrior, or hunter, whatever he may have been, I ascertained pretty quickly that he was no threat to me. He looked at me with warning, as if he was trying to threaten me into good behaviour with his eyes. In actuality, the man was almost half my height, and shriveled in comparison to my vast build. I hoped that he wasn't the scrappy type that would try to fight me because of my size. These types were rare, mostly because they only came from very well off villages of a moderate size, which seemed to give them some sort of strange inspiration. My guess was that this man wasn't among their ranks though. He seemed fearless, but not necessarily stupid. The man was well dressed, with a great deal of furs from rare and dangerous beasts, the kinds that I didn't imagine to see around those parts. In his long shaggy hair there was a variety of braiding and dreading done, filled with bones and feathers. Even his face mane, which was strong and thick, was decorated with teeth and claws, interwoven in his facial hair. With these fine decorations it was hard to imagine that this man didn't have a significant degree of clout in the village, meaning that he was more than the head warrior, but the leader and perhaps the shaman of these people. The question to me then became, who was this elderly man that translated what I was saying?

It wasn't worth questioning really, as I looked around it was obvious that the people here were a lot different than I was, especially from a cultural point of view. Maybe there was no hierarchy, a sort of anarchist system where each fends for their self and their family, yet looks out for the others in the tribe. At that point I had no clue, and all my thoughts were merely conjecture. At the end of our attempted conversation the warrior put his hand on my shoulder and motioned for me to follow him, a simple enough command that didn't require the elder's assistance to convey. He led me to one of the group shelters, a well-built thatch hut that even had exterior walls, a rare enough occurrence in these parts. There he motioned towards a giant patchwork of furs, a makeshift bed for a very large person. I laid on the furs, a good match for my shoulder width but a little too short. He gave me a pat on the leg where it extended off the edge of the bedding. I got up, and he grabbed the fur before bringing it over to the tanning station they had constructed. There he talked to a woman, who after their conversation starting to sew additional furs on the bottom of the bedding.

At that point I wasn't sure what I would do in that situation, they had accepted my presence, but at the same time I had to wonder whether they were trying to keep me as a member of their tribe, or merely a guest; the fact that they were creating a bed for a man my size, which I must admit, wouldn't be an easy task, told me that they were expecting me more than a couple of days. I began to think that perhaps the old man that I was conveying messages to had read my motions incorrectly, but I couldn't help but feel a bit flattered that they had so quickly accepted me. This was an unprecedented circumstance for me to say the least.

In my years on this Earth I had never been accepted by a whole group of people before, aside from the one that I was born in. Even as a youngster, the tribes nearby my own were distrustful of me because of my size, often viewing me as a threat more than a possible companion. It was strange to think

131

that this group, despite having known me for only a few hours saw my capabilities as a person, and not a danger. Now, feeling that I was effectively inaugurated, felt like a good time to introduce She, though I had a feeling she was nearer by than I knew. It was likely she had already scoped out the area and determined proper threats. It's entirely possible that the tribe itself had already seen her.

My feelings were proven correct, when I saw She roaming on the exterior of the village. The warrior that I had been with earlier was looking at her, so I motioned towards her to try and show that she was a friend. Humans, really every human I'd met found it quite hard to believe that She and I were companions. Creatures in our two species seemed to be made into enemies naturally, so it was a challenge to prove that we worked together. I was amazed then when the warrior simply turned away and walked on once She started to approach. Perhaps it was her peaceful gait, or perhaps the chief had a great ability when it came to dealing with other species. Either way for now I needed to show the rest of the tribe that She was to be trusted and could be considered a truly memorable element in the tribe.

Over the next half hour She and I walked throughout the village, her eyes almost always resting on me. Everything went over well, a surprising circumstance to say the least. I felt proud both of She and the people in the village, who had every right to distrust a creature like She. True, her kind was rarer in this part of the world, but not so rare that the tribe wouldn't have had a few encounters with them while they were out hunting. As to be expected there were a few awkward moments, her growling at a man who was leaving the shelter, and her finding out that I'd be staying in the camp, somewhere that she most assuredly would not be staying. At the end of it all though, she seemed rather fine with the idea.

Little did I know then, but this chance meeting would play a big role in my life, and what was to become of it. The two of us ended up staying there for years, becoming one with the community. I watched its members grow up into strong capable human beings. We would hunt and make merry, and a day without a full belly was a rare one to say the least. No matter how long I stayed there though, I always felt like a bit of an outsider. Only one of my children made it, though my partner had given birth to four. He was a boy by the name of River-Side, for that's where he was both born and conceived. Raising him came second only to my responsibility as the protector of the divine being.

As it became apparent to the people of the village the importance I placed in the creator, and as I grew to learn some of their language, others among them started to adopt to my ways, with more and more joining by the month. The only one who refused in their entirety to celebrate the creator's glory was the warrior chief. He claimed that even though the creator could be seen, and he admitted, even heard. It was his grandfather's gods that were the only truth in life. He figured it was his responsibility to protect their honour. The pyre that I had figured so odd on our approach was a religious monument and place of sacrifice; each day the man would place dead animals or people to send them into the heavens. A deity in the heavens was far too odd a concept for me, and it seemed many other members of the tribe.

For the longest time I let his derision against the creator slide, because the deity was telling me through my prayers that his gods were no threat to the strength of itself. I had been there for about four years when all of the sudden I couldn't help but shake this unnerving sense of danger. The only time that I ever felt such things was when She, or the creator was in trouble. I rushed out in the middle of the night to the altar that the tribesmen had built for the creator, and there I saw the chief, the man that everyone trusted most, hammering on the rock that encased the deity, cracking it ever further with each blow.

Though I respected the man and his authority, I had no hesitation in defending the creator over letting the scoundrel live. It was almost cute how he tried to attack me with his club, hitting me in the chest multiple times with wounds that would only inflict bruising. I yanked the club out of his hand and smashed his knee inwards, collapsing it and shattering the gentle bones that hid beneath the skin. As he fell backwards, collapsed into a heap of screams and ornate furs, I walked over kicked him in the head then stomped on his neck. The sound of the crack was deafening as the blood seemed to explode from the new orifices that I created on the sides of his throat. Though I couldn't see through his beard, I could only imagine that his neck's shape was now more akin to a lily pad than a log. I gave him mercy with that kick to the head, which almost certainly killed him before, giving him the mildest form of peace.

She must have heard the scuffle and she ran to my assistance. Everyone of able body was there; ready to kill me despite their religious devotion. The only one that wasn't there was River-Side and his mother. Seeing the carnage that was once their chief, most of the tribe folk ran away in fear before even confronting me, and the ones that stayed didn't last long facing the combined might of both She and I.

As I went down to the river to wash off the blood and viscera, I saw them in the distance, River-Side and his mother, escaping it all, heading towards the south, striving for warmth and peace. I had a feeling they weren't going to make it, but I prayed to the creator for them every day since.

"I told you we couldn't live among humans."

"Quiet yourself, wolf. At least we tried."

135

A Meeting with the King – Recurring Themes and a Good Friend

"A Meeting with the King" is a story about flawed men. The two main characters are entirely different people despite growing up together and coming from a similar circumstance. The big inspiration for this story came from my friendship with Mr. Standish, who has given timely and accurate advice whenever required. This story reminds me of our friendship, not just because of how I cherish it, but because it follows the nature of the tale as well.

The main character is loosely, and I mean very loosely, based on myself and what was once an inability to change. For a long time I felt as there were a serious lack of possibilities for me, wracked with mental illness, afraid to leave my home and desperate for companionship, I often felt as if life would remain a dry and motionless existence. In many ways it is my friendship with Rod that to me most represents my change as a person, not because he's the reason that I came out of my shell, but because he was the first friend that I made on my own. We had mutual friends, but at the time I didn't know that, I just knew Rod from his music and decided against the core of my disability that I would simply choose to become friends with him, and so I did. I was the one that chose to initiate first contact and repeat the process continuously until the point that we now sit, bordering on being the best of friends.

While I adore Rod and the friendship that he's given me, one might say that this story is a lot more about me, for my options at the time seemed to be either force the change or simply give up and remain at home for the rest of my days. I might say that I am both of the main characters, the knight being my old life and the king, the ultimatum that I had to eventually come across.

In the end I'm glad that I chose the freedom that comes along with social ability, as well as the great friendship with Rod that developed because of my own choices.

A Meeting with the King

They all laugh at me, the once great knight Godfrey Williamson. They laugh because of how I refuse to give up the past, an old man, still in knight's armour, who refuses to pick up one of those accursed boom sticks that make combat an utter embarrassment. What honour is there in simply pointing and shooting? It used to be that one's skill in combat came from their background, but now even the lowliest of peasant could kill me in a single blow. They've banned tourneys, and the sports that surround them, but there are still a few of us left, a few of us that refuse to leave the past behind.

I will admit, openly and without hesitation, that our methods are outdated. A king has more than enough rights to use a more effective means of waging war on the battlefield, but that does not mean that people should be allowed to ridicule us, the last greats of this generation. Around the whole of Europe they insult us, not just in my home. They write their comedies about the last of the knights, about how they're useless and deranged old fools. I remember only a few years earlier, we were the subject of great epics, where we'd save princesses and defeat dragons. What would Saint George think about all this? They forget we are among religious icons as well, chosen by the lord above. After all, I have yet to see a saint wielding a musket, or firing a cannon.

When I walk the streets in my armour, they all think it an act of comedy. They'll throw rotten food at me; I was even once stabbed in the back by a coward, though he quickly met the end of my mace, which shut them up pretty quick. I can't simply go around murdering everyone though, even I, a man who spent his life killing, am not that cold hearted. Plus, the king is starting to arm the peasants, who use their new found weaponry to hunt and protect their livestock from animals and thieves alike. It sickens me to see them more equal with men with wealth akin to myself. My children's children even have some friends amidst the rabble, thinking it to be a healthy exercise to understand the will of the small folk. Perhaps it is time that I change my ways, perhaps the era of the knight truly has come to an end, but I just can't bring myself to accept it. How I adored the thrill of the tourney back in my youth. I wasn't the wealthiest of men, yet I always succeeded in one category, the great melee. When there's a mace in my hand I was utterly unstoppable, that is before old age came to slow me down. Even now though, as a man in his twilight years, my muscles are still plenty strong, my body still prepared for a fight.

As old as I am, I was never alive in the great age of the knights. The age when stories about Arthur and his troop, who saved the weak and acted in chivalric majesty were flying off the shelves for anyone that had the capacity to read. This was the same time period when us knights would be the sole victors in

A Meeting with the King

wars, invincible war machines, made to slaughter anyone that came in our way. By the time I was growing the only place that you'd truly see knights was at tournaments. Cannons were already invented, the walls of Constantinople had already fallen, the crusades were centuries in the past. For most there was already a lack of nobility in knights by the time I became one, chivalry was a word that started to grind on people's ear drums as something that simply allowed knights additional rights that the rest of society didn't have. I still loved it though, and at least back then they would cheer for me, and show me respect in the streets. I was a big hit at tournaments "Godfrey the Breaker" they'd call me, for my famous move of breaking shields with my mace, or at least tearing them off the arms of my opponents.

Today, I am to meet the king, something that I haven't done since I was knighted decades ago. The king was old like me now, so I'm sure we'd have a lot to talk about. I remember once as I was walking the streets in my armour, one of the rabbles shouted out to me, "Off to meet the king, are ya?" If only he'd ask me now, that is if I didn't crush his skull like a grape. Every once in a while I'll hear them talking about me, whispering in hushed tones of fear; it made me proud more than anything. Even if they didn't respect me, at least they'd come to respect my martial abilities. There was one instance where an entire posse came to deal with me, wielding swords and guns, trying to catch me unawares. I swatted them all like flies though, five

140

of them in total. They couldn't even take down an old man. I forced them to come at me one at a time, using the doorway as a vantage point. My children were angry at me for the damage I'd done, leaving the manor in disarray. I was still the lord of this household though, and I'd be damned if they were to treat me with any disrespect.

As I made my way up to the king's palace, I looked at all the guards. Each of them dressed like pikemen, but with muskets instead of a hearty weapon. At least pikes were still being used on the front lines, which were about the only honourable aspect left in war. They all looked straight forward like true warriors, their eyes never dissenting to stare at me in my fully clad armour. I had grown up with the king, our father's being good friends, and he'd always commanded a great deal of respect, which I'm glad to see has yet to waiver. His name was King Roderick the Fourth, a mighty tower of a man, a contemporary Charlemagne based in both looks and ability to rule. He was the best king to come to power in my lifetime, having seen a total of four come and go, and I had a sinking feeling that he wasn't meeting with me to recall old times when we were children. I was causing a lot of trouble around his personal barony, even if in my defense I was always provoked.

The palace was just as majestic as I remembered, made in such a way that it displayed tradition and power at the same time. The entrance was a great timber portal with stone archways. The wood was decorated with the Albion coat of arms, and images of dragons, wolves and other perilous creatures. Chevron detailed the edges of the stone, chiseled decades prior, right before I was born. It was a huge project, that almost killed all the workers, so for some the palace was a beacon of cruelty, something that the current king has tried his best to rectify, returning the good name of his family that his grandfather soiled.

The inside of the palace was the pinnacle of high Gothic architecture; recent enough to keep up with the architectural style, yet traditional enough to display a seat of Royal majesty. I hadn't seen the inside of the palace since my teenage years, and it looked just as wonderful as before, and clean to an immaculate degree. As I moved through the palace, the members of court stared at me with a sense of indignation or disbelief. The court of Roderick the Fourth was known for its tact and cool manner, yet when confronted with the reality of a knight they lost all composure.

When I got to the throne room, I expected to find the king, but instead I was greeted by his steward. As soon as I came into the room the wiry man ran up to greet me. Sir Winston was a lot younger than the king himself, but he was known for his sage advice, not to mention his odd personality.

"Ah, Sir Williamson, yes, yes! The king has cleared his entire schedule today to spend the day conversing with you. For all intents and purposes, you are his majesty's most important visitor. In fact we had to turn down an ambassador from Brittany, so you should feel quite blessed. I must say, sir, I was never old enough to see the tourneys myself, but I've always found them fascinating. Unlike most of the people you'll find today, I know how respectful being a knight is, and I can't help but respect you for your choices! Enough about my own views though, you have a king to visit, come with me!"

As likely as it was that this steward was merely spinning diplomatic tales, I couldn't help but to smile at the compliment. It was far too rare to hear anything positive about myself these days, even at home I was an embarrassment, so a compliment, no matter how false the nature was always a treat.

As Sir Winston led me through the palace I managed to get a thorough look around the halls that I used to run around in as a child. I remember how Roderick and I would play games as his father, and then the crown prince would do his dealings with my father lord William, the duke at the time. After my father died the duchy fell apart in the hands of my elder brother, not that I would do any better, I was too busy playing in the tourneys to help my family out at all, something that haunted me for a long time. My brother decided to cut his losses, keeping the family's wealth instead of its honour and

A Meeting with the King

majesty. Now I was merely a rich man, with a few ties to royalty, nobody worthwhile of a king's full day.

Sir Winston was entirely accommodating of my desire to look around the castle, and even let me tell him the tales of an old man and his childhood adventures. I was amazed by how interested he was in so many of my stories, some of them he had even heard before. It was obvious to me then, that the king truly trusted this man, and that hopefully he trusted me. My whole life I've been particularly susceptible to good diplomacy, so soon enough Sir Winston had my full trust. It's hard to tell with diplomats whether they're truly honourable or just very good at seeming as such, but in truth, I wasn't a man in a position of power, so it didn't bother me either way, after all, I wasn't the one that needed to worry about the intentions of royalty.

After a complete walk down memory lane, filled with nostalgia, Sir Winston took me to the last stop, the king's chambers, where the man himself waited for me. The room that he took me to certainly wasn't the king's chambers that I had seen growing up, but it was the same room that Roderick slept in as a boy; a humble room for a humble man. The room was small, notably so, in fact it was smaller than my own room back at my manor. Aside from a large armoire there wasn't any sign of opulence, even the king's bed was made simply, as if it were crafted for a noble rather than the head of the royal household.

This was exactly like what I'd heard about Roderick, and indeed even though he was just a child, what I remembered about him.

He was by all means a man of simplicity with a keen mind for both strategy and diplomacy. In the two decades that he'd been king the nation flourished like it hasn't in a century, yet at the same time, he made no monumental moves, looking to avoid war instead of exploit it, keeping the treasury safe yet using the funds on the betterment of his people. Of the books I'd read I could imagine that he would be one of those greats who simply did his job so well that no one even noticed he was there. Only the cruelest, most selfish and most violent of kings tended to be immortalized, while great men like Roderick inspired people to be themselves and to write tales brewed from their own minds, rather than the acts of others. He was not the kind of man to have tales written about him, rather than having money spent on recalling his own deeds he would much rather spend his funds on bettering if not his family then the small folk. In every way he was superior to me, but of course he would never admit it.

He certainly didn't hide the fact that he was the king however, and his appearance in that room was one of majesty. Dressed in an ornate tunic with gold and silver clasps, fine leather trousers and boots, and a crown of solid gold made centuries prior, and designed to replicate the look of a forest wall. Luckily the man wasn't fully in his full kingly wear, or I'd have felt bad that he took all the time to put on such an outfit just to see me.

"Sir Godfrey, please come in. Sir Winston, you are free to leave, thank you." The wiry man turned on his heel and scurried out the door, shutting it gently behind him.

The king's presence was heavy, as if a wave was crashing on a cliff. I was overwhelmed at his words, as simple as they were. He looked to me, thinking I would be the one to start the conversation, and coming to the realization that I wouldn't, started.

"You know Godfrey, I often find myself relishing those childhood moments; the freedom, the wonder, that magical feeling of awe in discovering something new. I long for those feelings again, not often, but on occasion." He paused in the hope that I would say something, I didn't. "At the same time though, Godfrey, those things are in the past, gone forever, never to be seen again as much as we would like it to not be so. The past in provides a kind of beauty in nostalgia, even though I don't have much of a taste for sweets, the taste of a puff pastry brings back so many memories, which are often filled with you and the members of your house.

"There are many things in this life that I regret, after all nearly each decision I make could impact hundreds of people, but not doing something as your house fell to ruin is chief amongst. It haunts me, Godfrey, the memories of my small council telling me that your house was a lost cause, telling me to leave your brother to his whims despite my great desire to do the opposite. I listened to them then, I was new on the throne, and confused by my power. If I were to do it again I'd have that brother of yours thrown in shackles for what he did, who knows, maybe you'd be duke right now if I had made that choice. Alas, Godfrey, we come back to the nature of time. You are not a duke; you do not have the power or respect of a ruler. Why then must you act like you do? Sometimes I imagine that it's a means for you to get back at me for not saving your house back then. Sometimes I imagine that you still think of life as some sort of game to be played and won. There is no honour in what you do, Godfrey. Is that what you need to hear to end this charade? Do you need me to treat you like a dog and order you to behave?"

"Your Majesty, I—"

"No, you were given a chance to speak, and you disrespected me by not taking it. I am not that little boy any more, Godfrey, I won't play with you in the gardens. Despite what you might think, life is a challenge for all of us, as is change. I had no great design behind closing down the tourneys, I simply had to follow the will of the people, had to make compromises. Knights no longer act on the will of God, guns do. Your honour is no longer at stake, for you dismantled it long ago by killing my people. I've heard the reports, I know you were aggravated, and there were even a couple in which you had the right to act as you did, but for each other I'm afraid you need to be punished. Starting with the fact that you need to remove that damned armour."

Two armed guards entered the room, wearing cotton clothing and wielding muskets. I had no fear of these men, they were young, but they didn't have the training that I did. If it came down to it, I would be able to fight them perfectly well, but alas, I don't think it would come to that. When it came down to it, it was time for me to give up the old ways. My honour was not worth disgracing my king.

Slowly I removed my armour, defeated in both spirit and mind. I handed the two men the pieces as I removed them. "I am sorry, Your Majesty. You're right, for what is the honour of a man worth if he would kill out of rage alone. I just, I was never able to give up on those days, I could never come to the conclusion that life was over for me. There is nothing for me to do anymore, I'm an old man, useless and defeated. That's what you wanted isn't it, to crush my spirits, like I crushed the skulls of all those lowly peasants." What was once indignation and fear was turning into rage. I would not be so easily defeated by a man who gave no honour to the wealthy, no special resources. "You put their lives equal to mine, your childhood friend? Where's the honour in that? Maybe," I started to put my armour back on wrenching it from the guards. "Maybe, there's nothing left for my kind in this world, but I'll be damned if I'm going to let some peasant loving caveman like yourself treat me as such. Give me that damned greave, you scoundrel! I'm leaving this damned palace with my honour intact, whether I'm dead or alive, I wish the same could be said for you."

The king glared at me, my words had clearly had their effect. "Let's see what honour you have as another corpse at the bottom of the river, which is where you'll end up with words like that." The two guards stepped forward, muskets at the ready.

"I would rather die than spend another moment with a traitorous heathen like you. You were a good child, and a worthwhile king, but as a man, you're feeble."

The king nodded to the men who filled my exposed back with musket balls. The cowards didn't even have the audacity to hit me in the armour that I so loved. As I lay there dying, the king pulled something off of the wall. It was my family crest, back when we were still a royal house. "Do not worry, Godfrey, I'll have this buried with you. You may have cursed my name on this day, but I have nothing against that child that used to play with me in the gardens. You won't be fish food, but a revered soldier."

With that came my last breath, it was one of satisfaction.

The Tomb – A Tribute to a Singular Topic

I absolutely adore the works of H.P. Lovecraft. In my opinion he is the utter emperor of the short story, and the horror novella. He was a flawed man to be sure; afraid, neurotic and just downright evil in many respects, but his skill can't be ignored.

Out of all the stories I've ever written this one took the longest to compose, I had to try to enter the man's mindset as well as I could while at the same time maintaining my own style. There's really not much to say about this story, I'm afraid. Its purpose is quite singular and I kind of adore it, especially the ending. Enjoy!

The Tomb

Dilapidated ruins of a small community littered the landscape, with only a few scarce occupants who maintained the ever present sense of dread that filled the town. The people there were deformed both physically and mentally due to generations of inbreeding and an absence of even the slightest semblance of health care. In this town amongst the overgrown flora, broken down relics and ferocious marshland beasts, there was a cemetery known for being even more mysterious than the town itself.

The cemetery's most well-known resident was the cultist Zadok Marsh who almost single- handedly created the infamy of the town that led to its eventual downfall. Famous for his numerous attempts to resurrect various creatures and human spirits associated with the occult, Zadok and his brutality died with the blood of dozens of innocent humans and creatures on his hands. This event happened long ago, centuries had gone by that in most cases would clean the town's reputation and return it to normal, but this case was very different. Once a year every year, someone would disappear, the day varied but it would always happen in the middle of the night when people were expecting it least. People, mostly young, would simply walk out of the house never to be seen again.

The Tomb

This story is that of an intrepid investigator and his attempt to solve a mystery that was simply not meant to be solved. A skeptic by nature, Howard Armitage did not believe in anything supernatural, he, like his biologist father, believed that everything in life could be explained using science and good old-fashioned human logic. Little did Howard know that he was about to run into the greatest opposition to human logic ever seen by man.

Upon reaching the town Howard was greeted grimly by the gatekeeper who guarded the only way in or out of that macabre place. The gate creaked open, clearing the ground behind it of the thick layer of moss and the abhorred masses of fungi that had sprouted up between the cracked road. As Howard began to drive through the gate the gatekeeper slapped the hood of his automobile with his walking stick before positioning himself on the other side of Howard's window.

Howard rolled down the window for the frail thick-lipped man beside his car, "Can I help you, friend?" The man stared at Howard looking up and down his face. He then proceeded to shove his head through Howard's window, supposedly to get a better look inside. Before pulling his head back out the man looked directly into Howard's eyes and let out a raspy grunt. Once the man had made his way out of the window he looked at Howard one more time before slapping his stick against the hood once again. Howard took this as a sign that he was free to go.

In his many years as an investigator Howard had seen his fair share of small rundown communities, so he found himself quite prepared for the town's less than pleasant demeanor, but as soon as he saw that gatekeeper he knew he wasn't prepared for the people he would meet. Howard already had some knowledge of this case, he knew that the people of the town blamed the disappearances on the dead cult ruler and had come to the assumption that either people were simply leaving without anyone noticing or there was a group of serial kidnappers and possibly murderers in the town. By reviewing the case file it was a certain truth to him that it must be a group behind these misdeeds, mostly due to how long these disappearances had been going on, but there were other factors as well that led to the fact that this was a group of assailants.

This town was known for its xenophobia, so Howard had to make a noticeable presence before he himself disappeared. He had dealt with gated communities before so he knew the best place to dissolve what might otherwise be a threatening presence to the townsfolk was to head to the seat of authority in the area, in this case the town hall.

Town hall unlike every other spot in the town was actually quite well maintained. Its windows were clear, its roof wasn't ridden with holes and rotten shingles, and its walls, which were covered in a modern siding, remained unbent. Even with all the seemingly normalized attributes, town hall made Howard feel quite wary of his surroundings, there was something not quite right about this building; it reeked of schemes, plotting and danger. The interior of the town hall matched the outside, it was far from being able to be described as lavish, but the presence of cleanliness and regular maintenance was apparent and oddly discomforting.

As Howard approached the front desk the young woman sitting behind it raised her head and as her eyes met Howard's her face displayed a sense of great confusion, Howard supposed that she wasn't used to seeing people that she didn't know. Howard stood in front of the desk looking at the woman who had since diverted her attention to filing her finger nails which were coated with a cracked and blotchy paint job that was either quite old or horribly done.

"Excuse me, miss?" The woman looked up at Howard for a second time, and as it had been before when she met his eyes confusion flowed over her facial features. Howard had no idea what to think of it, how could woman be confused of him again? She had seen him what must have been less than ten seconds prior. This time the woman did not avert her gaze from Howard, but much like the gatekeeper she had yet to say a word. "I was wondering if there was some sort of visitor's pass. I'm here to investigate some crimes and have been given authority by the province to do so."

"Visitor's pass? Never had no need for them, ain't got no visitors," the young woman's language was appalling, she could barely string together the sentence she just spoke, so Howard decided there was no use in questioning her further, but he still needed some sort of recognition that he was allowed to be there, so he pressed on.

"Well, do you have anything that could identify the fact that I'm allowed to be here?"

"I just said we got a visitor's pass. Haven't ya heard of a two time negative? Damn, boy, you need some education. Let me go find it for ya, though it might take me awhile 'cause I ain't got a clue where it would be."

The young woman lurched off into a room situated behind her desk. Howard noticed her labored walk, which seemed to be one of disfigurement rather than pain. As he waited for her return he looked to the wall behind him. Above the door that he had entered there were a number of portraits of what he assumed were mayors of the city. The portraits hung in chronological order from left to right and as the portraits went down the line the two distinctly different characteristics were the progressively diminishing amounts of facial hair from portrait to portrait and a decay in the quality of the painting itself, with the one on the far left looking like the work of a Renaissance master and the one on the far right looking like it was painted by a slightly practiced prepubescent child.

Nearly an hour had passed before the young woman returned. Howard had spent that time perusing the foyer, which held a considerable amount of information in the books available to the public, whose shelves were littering the east wall. Through these books Howard was able to determine the population of the town, which was recorded to be 812 when the last count took place three months prior. He also found that these books proved to be quite a valuable source of information when it came to the town's occult history, and he decided that he would ask if he could borrow a couple for his own research.

"Here ya go, stranger, the visitor pass. Damned thing was 'idden up on the top of a shelf, it was the last place available for me to look and when I got a chair to peek up 'ere I was like 'Lord, if that ain't it there!' I mean, what are the chances of that?!"

"Well, thank you very much. I'm sorry that I put you through all the trouble of finding it, but I was also wondering if I could borrow some of those books over there, for research purposes." Howard motioned over to the books.

"Hm, I suppose ya could, but I ain't sure of it. In my time here I've never had someone actually take those books out of the building. Then again I've never actually seen anyone read them, so I say it's fine, but know that if this gets me in some sort of trouble I'll be putting all the blame on you."

"I don't mean to put you in that sort of position. Is there possibly someone else that works here that I could speak to directly about it, your supervisor perhaps?"

"Now listen here," the woman seemed very angry, "I'm my own boss around 'ere and if I say you can borrow 'em then you better well borrow 'em. Get yer books and get the hell out of here stranger. Take yer God-damned visitor pass with ya."

Needless to say Howard was confused by the woman's quick change in demeanor, but he took her advice, grabbed everything he needed and with one final inspection of the mayors' portraits he got "the hell out of there." Before he headed out to his next destination, the cemetery, Howard decided to do a little research in the car. He cracked open the book that he found provided the most information on the town's cultist history and gave a quick skim through the chapters that would be the most use to him on his investigation.

After a good twenty minutes of reading Howard came to a few very helpful conclusions; the town was obsessed with the occult, Zadok Marsh was viewed as an upstanding member of the community despite all the killings, people were generally fine with their loved ones disappearing and the town had a history of mistreating visitors. After referencing the other books he determined these facts were apparent in all of them, and he had begun to finally get a small picture of how this town operates.

What was most interesting to him is that the books in themselves provided a different picture of the town. Though they were only written a couple of years prior the language in them was immaculate, well versed and painstakingly cited. The sole author, a Dr. Deborah Bish, was a resident. The book went as far as to provide her address. Though, it was already in Howard's mind to visit the cemetery, he now had another visit to make afterwards. Two leads are better than one.

The cemetery, named "Marshland Graveyard" was an odd place, much akin to the rest of the town. The grass was so high it went halfway up Howard's shins, most of the tombstones had fallen over or been broken, and some of the graves were so shallow you could make out the shape of the coffin if you looked close enough. By provincial law it was illegal to keep such a sacred public space in disarray, something that Howard noted, but figured he'd never act on. The town had enough problems as it was.

Amongst all the shattered gravestones and weed infested grass lay a number of structures, all as dilapidated as the rest of the area, except for one, a great tomb, standing at least four meters tall, and maybe twice as long, the building was monstrous, far too large for one person; who it belonged to was obvious as soon as Howard saw the building, it must be the tomb of the revered Zadok Marsh. He could only hope that the whole graveyard wasn't named after the man.

Making his way to the tomb, Howard found that the building was surrounded by about a dozen other graves, all of which were also kept in as best condition as could be imagined for their age. Though time had worn down most of the names to near illegibility there was a few that stuck out to Howard. Tallduc and Travet, two names that he had seen hanging below the portraits in town hall. They must've been the names of the mayors long past, although there were far less graves here than there were portraits, so the tradition must have died out at some point. Howard made a note of this in his journal, deciding that he should look up the location of the mayors that weren't among these dozen or so. For now though, it was time to make his way into the tomb.

The stench of dust and the thick feeling in the air was palpable. Although the outside was well taken care of, it seems the same couldn't be said for the inside. Compared to the other graves in the cemetery it was clear that this area wasn't left in complete disarray. Howard guessed that it was cleaned every few months or so. In the center of the room lying lengthwise was a massive coffin, with a great shrine located right behind it.

The Tomb

Both the walls were completely filled with corpses, aligned like the catacombs one might see beneath a Roman temple. None of these corpses were covered up, their bodies sitting loose with scraps of clothing being the only thing that covered the skeletal remains. None of them even went named, but it was evident who was situated in the center of the room.

Etched deeply into the stone sarcophagus were the words "ZADOK MARSH, FATHER OF MANY AND SPIRITUAL KING OF THE PEOPLE". Aside from words the sarcophagus was also covered in immaculate decorative patterns, which lay perfectly symmetrical on either side, some key pieces were even inlaid with silver. The fact that this grave was never robbed shows just how much the town cared, or feared the menace of this man. The conclusion came to Howard that as a foreigner to the town he ought to get out of this vicinity quickly, as there was no doubt in his mind that there had to be someone guarding the precious elements of the tomb. Before he left he hurried to take some quick pictures, then rushed out. Luckily no one was out there waiting for him.

Given the state of the cemetery, Howard decided his best course of action was to do some research on the location of the various plots for the mayors before he simply began to look for them himself. Although the graveyard was in a terrible shape, it was the biggest fixture in the town by far, at least from what Howard had seen. He did notice before he left, the most recent additions to the cemetery, all the members of the same family the "Potence" family, an odd name, and even an odder circumstance. Aside from their names and death dates, under each name it said "DIED" as if there was a possibility that living people could be buried in the cemetery. An even odder element was how the stones were marked, which seemed to have been done crudely by a file of some sort, making the final result look similar to the writing of a child.

The address of Dr. Deborah Bish led to a rundown manor of formidable size. Like most other buildings in the town this one looked as if it was rotting away, and it was astounding that such a building was still standing. As Howard stood waiting at the door, hoping that someone would respond to his knocking, an older man walked by.

"What are ya up to? Ain't nobody home in that old place, boy."

"You aren't using a double negative are you?"

"A double what? The hell kind of language is that, son. There ain't a soul in there, old doctor Bish done died a good old few months ago."

"Ah, I'm sorry to hear that, I was just looking for some information on the town, and hoping she'd be able to provide some."

The Tomb

"That she would've stranger, she was the only type of folk that fit in with the rest of the world around here. Good lass she was, a shame. I tell you what, I'm the landlord of this place, I'll let ya in to take a look around, ya just gotta take lots of care." The old man shambled up to the door, almost tripping over himself a few times on his way. It was hard to tell if he was drunk or disabled, but Howard had a feeling that it was a bit of both.

Unlocking the door, the man turned to Howard, "I oughta warn ya, she's still in there."

"What do you mean, who's still in there?"

"Deborah, her corpse is still in there. Cemetery's full so they're just leaving her to rot, the bastards."

"Wait, you're telling me that there's a woman's corpse in there? Why not bury her in the backyard? That's beyond disgusting, indecent and not to mention unsanitary." Numb with shock, Howard lost all his tact. "You freaks here have to do something about all this vile nonsense. What is wrong with you people?!"

The old man didn't even have time to respond before Howard started to wander away, running as fast he could wiping the fear off of his face. He didn't stop running until he found a big stone by the roadside that he could sit on to get some peace. It had been less than a day and already this place was starting to get to him. He decided that from here on out

he'd have to develop harder skin. Never before in his life had he
been to such a disturbing and backwards place, but he was the
visitor here, and he had a job to do.

It was a few minutes until he came back to doctor Bish's
house, figuring that the best way to develop a resistance to all
this madness was to drown in it. The old man was still waiting
there for him. "I apologize for that, you simply caught me
unprepared."

"Ah, it ain't a worry, boy. I'll keep it between the two of
us." As he unlocked the door, which took a while given his
arthritic fingers, he recalled his memories of when he was
younger. "You know, when I was growing up a good 70 years
ago now, this place was a lot saner. They'll tell you, detective-
That's what you are, right? Yeah, well they'll tell you that these
disappearances have been going on since the beginning of time,
ever since that Marsh freak infected these lands. That just ain't
true though, it goes just as far back as anyone can remember, or
at least cares to.

"Yep, back when I was a kid this was a nice place,
peaceful with a little tourism from the people that enjoy the
occult, kind of like that witch town in the States. It wasn't 'til
about 65 years ago that things started to fall apart. It just
started with a bit of vandalism, but escalated quickly into the
murder of that Higgins boy. People stopped coming by around

then, and the town began to devolve into this cult mindset, the likes I ain't seen before, I tell ya." The door, unlocked, threw itself open. "Anyhow, that's all I oughta tell ya, the powers that be around here aren't too keen on loose lips, they sink ships and all that."

Howard thanked the man for the information and apologized once again before heading into the building. He had expected a terrible stench, but inside it merely smelt musty and degenerated, like wet wood in an attic. The whole of the building was a feast for the senses, inside lay a veritable hoard of the town's artifacts, from maps to centuries old farm equipment and other technologies. Everything was preserved in glass cases, all thinly coated in a layer of dust; just enough to make it difficult to make out what was inside each one. Still in a tizzy, Howard unveiled one of them thinking it would be a human head, but turned out to be a bowling ball.

Aside from the well-kept artifacts the house was in utter shambles. Decades if not more of neglect was evident in the rotten walls and torn floorboards. Even some of the exterior walls would wobble when Howard leaned against them. He was confused as to how someone that wrote such an intellectual tome could live in such decay for so long, though intellect didn't always secure an idea of common sense he supposed. Eventually Howard came to find a clue, a massive book written by the doctor herself on the cult practices that took place in the town. He found it in the woman's study sitting open on a big mahogany desk, luckily not eaten by termites. What was even luckier than the quality of the book was the fact that he had yet to come into contact with the apparent corpse that lay waiting as a horrific surprise.

As Howard began to go upstairs to the second of three floors the scents began to hit him. The smell not just of rot, but of urine and feces struck him as his head went above the top of the stairs. Its rancid nature was so abhorrent that Howard took this as a sign to get out of there with sanity he had intact, until he heard a voice.

"Hello?" it said, deep and raspy, but unmistakably female. "Are you there or am I hearing things?" Whatever it was spoke slowly and without confidence in the pronunciation of its own words, as if it were surprised that it was talking at all. "Did you need something?"

As Howard was staring down the upstairs hallway, some sort of limb, unidentifiable, slowly protruded from the door at the end. It looked wooden, covered in a type of moss, and shining with rot. Without notice the limb lunged out cracked into the floor board and began dragging out what could only be described as a monstrosity. It had the face of a middle-aged woman, jaw half torn off with a body that could be described as a tangle of wood, tentacles and fur.

The Tomb

"Ah, so there is someone there. Come closer, I haven't seen anyone in ages." As she saw Howard her words gained more confidence and she spoke in almost an ordinary cadence, if it wasn't for the horrific nature of her voice. As Howard heard more, he realized it wasn't raspy as much as it was electronic, shuttering and full of a droning undercurrent more related to static than anything else. "My name is Deborah. I... apologize for the mess; it's hard to get around you see." Every once in a while globs of saliva would pour out of her dislocated jaw, which shook as she spoke. It was obvious where the smell was coming from. Aside from her terrifying appearance the beast had the wherewithal to stay put, possibly knowing the horrifying nature of her existence. "You must have questions."

Howard was motionless, struck by every fear that he'd ever had at once, but once he regained the ability to use his legs he got out of there as fast as he could, and I don't just mean the house, he left the town, then the state, then the country. He spent the rest of his life as a disturbed man who couldn't keep a job. He was known as the man that wandered the streets of Scotland, murmuring about a "tree woman" and "that damned old man."

About the Author

Erik Upper is a Niagara Falls native with an obsession for history. He also enjoys all things cold, as can be seen by how often his stories take place in tundra.

Easily described as an eccentric, Erik is weird by nature and loves all things strange. After becoming fixated on the works of H.P. Lovecraft and Cormac McCarthy he decided to have his own try at the writing game, bringing his personal oddities with him.

Sporting a top hat and speaking with a dialect similar to a Victorian gentleman, Erik is hard to miss, even with his short stature.

Made in the USA
Charleston, SC
06 June 2016